MEMORY
MAKERS

SCRAPBOOK
EMBELLISHMENTS

**MEMORY
MAKERS
BOOKS**

Executive Editor   Kerry Arquette   Founder Michele Gerbrandt

Art Director Andrea Zocchi

Designer Nick Nyffeler

Craft Editor Jodi Amidei

Art Acquisitions Editor Janetta Wieneke

Photographer Ken Trujillo

Contributing Photographer Brenda Martinez

Contributing Writer Kelly Angard

Editorial Support Emily Curry Hitchingham, MaryJo Regier, Dena Twinem

Memory Makers® Scrapbook Embellishments (*The Masters Series*)

Published by Memory Makers Books, an imprint of F & W Publications, Inc.

12365 Huron Street, Suite 500, Denver, CO 80234

Phone 1-800-254-9124

First edition. Printed in Singapore.

08 07 06 05 04 5 4 3 2 1

Library of Congress Cataloging-in-Publication Data

Scrapbook embellishments.
     p. cm.
   Includes index.
   ISBN 1-892127-31-8
   1. Photograph albums. 2. Photographs--Conservation and restoration. 3. Scrapbooks. 4.
   Decoration and ornament. 5. Handicraft. I. Memory Makers Books.

   TR465.S3934 2003
   745.593--dc22

                                                        2003065109

Distributed to trade and art markets by

F & W Publications, Inc.

4700 East Galbraith Road, Cincinnati, OH 45236

Phone 1-800-289-0963

ISBN 1-892127-31-8

Memory Makers Books is the home of *Memory Makers*, the scrapbook magazine dedicated to educating and inspiring scrapbookers. To subscribe, or for more information, call 1-800-366-6465. Visit us on the Internet at www.memorymakersmagazine.com.

Thank you to this exceptionally talented group of artists, our 2003 Memory Makers Masters, who have shared their art with scrapbookers around the world. You are an inspiration. We are privileged to showcase your work.

The Editors of Memory Makers Books

Table of Contents

10 Organics

Bring nature to your pages with dried flowers and leaves, jute or hemp string, rocks, spanish moss, leather, wood, clay tiles, seeds, feathers, sea glass, raffia, pine needles, wheat straw, twigs and other elements from the great outdoors.

30 Textiles

Add texture, richness and depth to your scrapbook pages through the use of textiles— including nubby cotton or linen, shiny satin, the jewel or earth tones of fibers—twisted, tied or strung across a page. For a homey feel, a back-to-roots essence, textiles are the embellishment of choice.

52 Baubles

Dress up a page with jewelry that turns an everyday ensemble into something special. Tiny mico beads, glass pebbles, glitter and tinsel as well as other shiny embellishments catch the eye. String them, glue them to photos or photo mats for stunning effects.

74 Paper Crafts

With hundreds of colors and countless prints and textures, paper can be used to create an endless variety of scrapbook embellishments. Learn to weave, fold, punch, pleat, quill, cut and tear paper to create decorative elements for any page theme.

96 Metallics

Shiny, warm, malleable metals bring an earthy or masculine feel to many scrapbook pages. Perfect for tags, titles, journaling and photo corners, or used in the form of metal wire which is twisted and strung with beads, metallics are a wonderful addition to a scrapbooker's tool box.

Meet the Memory Makers Masters

Brandi Ginn

Although Brandi Ginn began scrapbooking as a child, married life and motherhood proved to be the motivation for her taking up the craft on a consistent basis four years ago. For Brandi, scrapbooking is the natural form for her interests in photography and the overall creative process to take. As Brandi describes, scrapbooking affords her the rewarding and unique opportunity to create something meaningful and lasting from the perspective of both an artist and mother. "There's a great sense of accomplishment that comes from preserving our family's history." Describing her style as fairly traditional, Brandi most enjoys documenting the life and times of her family in her scrapbook pages. Evolving as a crafter and pushing herself to turn out innovative work characterizes Brandi's experience as a Memory Makers Master. When not conceptualizing her next layout, Brandi is at work as a freelance writer and designer, and lives in Lafayette, Colorado, with husband Nathan and daughters Alexa and Brinley.

Katherine Brooks

Katherine began scrapbooking six years ago after the birth of her daughter. Initially scrapbooking with the primary purpose of documenting her family's overall history and special times, Katherine soon discovered scrapbooking to be the perfect outlet for creative expression. Describing her style and approach to scrapbooking, Katherine says, "I like adding simple detail to my layouts. As for my style, I love country décor and find that it transfers into my layouts." A proud mom, Katherine most enjoys creating layouts of her family. For the sake of her children, she strives to scrapbook more about herself. For Katherine, being a Memory Makers Master has given her an opportunity to correspond with other women who share her enthusiasm for the craft, and has led to new friendships. When not scrapbooking, Katherine is busy as an instructor and product designer for Deluxe Designs, and has recently released an idea book titled, *Tagging Along*. Katherine lives in Gilbert, Arizona, with husband John and children Meghan and Matt.

Valerie Barton

A scrapbooker for four years, Valerie Barton began with the intention of preserving her children's school memories in an album, a task which eventually evolved into a full-blown passion and creative outlet. Valerie cites the therapeutic nature of scrapbooking and its impact on the positive elements in life. In her own words, "If I'm having a bad day, all I have to do is work on my pages." Characterizing herself as an "out-of-the-box" scrapbooker, Valerie adds that her approach to scrapbooking favors the dimensional, where layers, paper craft and fibers create texture and dimension that are often considered "shabby chic." Being a Memory Makers Master for Valerie has meant having the opportunity to interact with other women who have the same passion. She says being a Master has also been motivation for her to strive to become a better journaler. When not hard at work scrapbooking, Valerie works as an elementary school counselor in Flowood, Mississippi where she lives with husband Mark, daughter Kaitlyn and son Addison.

Diana Hudson

Diana Hudson began scrapbooking 11 years ago, after the arrival of her first child. Recognizing the opportunity to combine her interests in needlework, paper art and journaling, Diana began scrapbooking in order to create timeless keepsakes for future generations of her family. For Diana, scrapbooking provides a unique opportunity to remember what is important and share it with others, particularly through journaling. "The photos are a treasure, but the written word is equally important to me," says Diana. Describing her style as clean, classic, as well as eclectic, Diana enjoys trying new styles in order to continuously evolve as a scrapbooker. As a Memory Makers Master, Diana has appreciated the friendships forged with other Masters who, like her, have viewed the experience as a springboard for exploring new products and techniques. In addition to her artistic endeavors, Diana is a stay-at-home mom who revels in caring for her family. She lives in Bakersfield, California, with husband Curtis and children Ryan and Sydney.

Torrey Miller

Torrey Miller has been scrapbooking for the past three and a half years, after having been invited by a friend to a crop. Instantly, the craft became the creative solution for artistically uniting all the things Torrey enjoys best. In her own words, "Scrapbooking offers me a single medium in which I can expressively combine my poetry, photography, art and writing, all in a beautiful package." A self-described "artsy" and "eclectic" scrapbooker, Torrey particularly enjoys scrapbooking loved ones as well as the scenic photographs she takes. Over the course of her Memory Makers Masters tenure, Torrey says that in addition to building friendships, she has been challenged to scrap outside her comfort zone and experiment more in her layouts, leading to a willingness to try most any technique. When not planning her next project, Torrey works as a pediatric registered nurse and freelance writer, and enjoys the creative influences of friends and family members. Torrey lives in Thornton, Colorado.

Diana Graham

Diana Graham's interest in scrapbooking actually began more as an obsession with scrapbooking products than with scrapbooking itself. Until being invited to a crop by a local scrapbook store owner, Diana was content with simply shopping for the embellishments that would later adorn her pages. "I was in love with picking out paper and stickers and new gadgets and tools," she says. Four years later, Diana now enjoys scrapbooking for the relationships it promotes, as well as the smiles on her children's faces when they look at her scrapbooks. In describing her style and approach to scrapbooking, Diana says she favors using a lot of product on her pages. She says that being a Memory Makers Master has given her the opportunity to explore new themes and products, and the Masters challenges have forced her to push her creativity to new levels. In addition to to her crafting endeavors, Diana is a stay-at-home mom who lives in Barington, Illinois, with husband Brad and children Jeremy and Ella.

Kelli Noto

Having scrapbooked in high school, Kelli Noto renewed her interest in the craft after the arrival of her first child 11 years ago. For Kelli, her scrapbooking is a tribute to her children as well as a special form of family documentation for future generations. In characterizing her style, Kelli notes that her color choices and favoring of bold, graphic lines are the result of the masculine influences from raising two sons. As for her approach, Kelli says, "I believe that scrapbook pages should start with the photos. I try to keep my pages photocentric and use embellishments only as enhancements." Kelli's most prized photo opportunities and favorite scrapbooking subjects are catching her children hard at play and engaged in sports. As a Memory Makers Master, Kelli has enjoyed exchanging techniques with her newfound friends and fellow Masters artists, and has been inspired to continuously evolve in page design. In addition to being a busy scrapbooker, Kelli owns a photography business and lives in Centennial, Colorado, with husband John and children Eric and Kevin.

Heidi Schueller

Having kept a scrapbook during her high school and college years, Heidi Schueller returned to her former hobby two and a half years ago while working as a Creative Memories consultant. It was this experience that Heidi says instigated her passion for "modern" scrapbooking and her enthusiasm for its resurgence. Characterizing her approach to scrapbooking as "resourceful," Heidi always strives for originality in her layouts and works to create pages that invite personal interpretation. "When people look at my pages, I want the photos and artwork to tell a story. The whole page should give an emotion and feeling to the onlooker," says Heidi. As for favorite scrapbooking subjects, Heidi enjoys creating layouts based on her children and her travels. As a Memory Makers Master, Heidi has most appreciated the additional opportunities to create new art based on the Master's challenges, meeting her fellow Masters, and serving as a Camp Memory Makers instructor. When not working at her craft, Heidi is a stay-at-home mom and scrapbook instructor and lives in Waukesha, Wisconsin, with husband Bill and daughters Isabel and Claudia.

Trudy Sigurdson

Trudy Sigurdson began scrapbooking two and a half years ago after a trip to replenish her rubber stamping supplies led her into a scrapbooking store. She was hooked after taking one class. Now a scrapbook designer and instructor, Trudy describes her style of scrapbooking as textured and dimensional, where her love for paper scrunching, distressing, and machine sewing all converge. In describing her approach of utilizing fewer photos and incorporating reflective journaling, Trudy says, "I think that I am more of an emotional scrapbooker than an event scrapbooker. I prefer to write and record poems or quotes that show how much I love my children." According to Trudy, being a Memory Makers Master has pushed her creatively, leading her to new products and the assignments have helped her expand her style. In addition to her regular teaching and designing, Trudy served as a Camp Memory Makers instructor in the summer of 2003. Trudy lives in Victoria, British Columbia, with children Aysha and Alex.

Holle Wiktorek

A scrapbooker since high school, Holle Wiktorek has 13 years of scrapbooking and five years of teaching scrapbook classes to her credit. What began as a school assignment grew into a much-loved pastime for documenting both life-changing and everyday events. Holle notes that scrapbooking has become a way for her to close the distance between far away friends and family, namely her often-deployed U.S. Army officer husband. "When my husband is deployed, scrapbooking keeps us close as I relive our moments together," says Holle. Hesitant to categorize her scrapbooking style due to its constant evolution, Holle continuously works to find new techniques using paper tearing and chalking and her favorite products of cardstock and embellishments. As a Memory Makers Master, Holle has challenged herself to try new products and improve with each featured layout, enjoying the exchange of ideas with fellow Masters. In addition to instructing scrapbook classes, Holle is a public school teacher and lives in Clarksville, Tennessee, with her husband, Thomas.

Embellishments Library

The scrapbooker who was once concerned about how to fill a white page need worry no longer. The exponential growth of scrapbooking has resulted in a plethora of extraordinary embellishments that turn one-dimensional layouts into canvases of creative expression. Scrapbook toolboxes now hold beautiful threads, sparkling beads, whimsical buttons and much more. While not all embellishments are safe to bring into contact with photos and memorabilia, it is still possible to place them on pages in ways that avoid close proximity, or to encase them in pockets, 3-D keepers and shaker boxes. Enjoy exploring both design possibilities and the array of stunning embellishments on the market today.

Organics

Hemp, jute and string were the forerunners when it came to organic embellishing. The lumpy nature of these embellishments concerned some scrapbookers, however. As scrapbooks became more 3-D, these products were perceived as less obtrusive. They were joined by objects such as pressed flowers and leaves, skeleton leaves, grasses, shells and seeds. In the future more people may wish to press their own flowers and leaves or pound flowers into pulpy colorants for shadowing and enhancing art. Organics are perfect embellishments for earthy pages including vacation and outdoor themes and they are sure to fit in well on "altered" page collage-like spreads.

Textiles

Years ago, the recognition that fabrics and sewing techniques could support scrapbook page themes led scrapbookers to create faux sewing in their albums. However, rather than reach for true sewing supplies, they "quilted" together pieces of paper and created penned "stitch" lines. More recently scrapbook artists have been browsing their local fabric stores for supplies such as fabrics, ribbons, zippers, embroidery floss, threads and quilting patterns. The result? Scrapbook pages with softer edges, more dimension, a homey feel and texture to spare.

Baubles

While glitter has found a home on scrapbook pages for some years, other forms of glitz such as beads, tinsel and sequins are more recent additions to the scrapbook toolbox. Tiny micro beads and marbles, sequins, glass pebbles, rhinestones, gems and other decorative elements add sparkle as well as dimension to today's pages. Scrapbookers continue to expand, visiting non-scrapbook related aisles in their hobby stores for inspiration and products that push the envelope such as tiles and mirrors. While no one can predict exactly what the future holds, many scrapbook professionals expect to see increasingly intricate beadwork designs on pages.

Paper

Paper, in all its variations, is a staple of scrapbooking. While today's scrapbookers continue to reach for cardstock and patterned papers, they are growing increasingly excited about the novelty and specialty papers such as mulberry, waushi, velvets, embossed and metallic papers. They are tearing, sculpting, folding, ironing, pleating, wetting, painting, crimping and embossing them to create awesome embellishments for pages across all themes. In looking forward, scrapbookers are also looking back toward ancient paper arts such as origami and iris folding to embellish their pages. All it takes is a bit of research and daring.

Metallics

Metallic papers, first popular a handful of years ago, opened the door for the use of other metallics on scrapbook pages. They were followed by freeform wire titles and embellishments, created by wrapping thin wire around pegs. Paper clips, eyelets, brads and page jewelry as well as metallic leafing products have become increasingly popular to dress up elegant layouts. Many of the available metallics have been made in silver but the future is sure to offer more gold, copper and bronze-colored embellishments as well as adhesives created specifically to hold them to pages.

To my Beautiful Daughter

I looked at you today and saw
the same beautiful eyes
that looked at me with love when
you were a baby.
I looked at you today and saw the same beautiful
mouth that made me cry
when you first smiled at me when
you were a baby.
It was not long ago that I
held you in my arms
long after you fell asleep and I just kept
rocking you all night long.
I looked at you today and saw my beautiful
daughter no longer a baby
but a beautiful person with a full range of
emotions and feelings and ideas and goals.
Every day is exciting as I continue
to watch you grow.
And I want you to always know that
in good and bad times I will love you
and that no matter what you do
or how you think or what you say
you can depend on my support, guidance
friendship and love every minute of every day.
I love being your mother.

April 2003

Aysha

Organics

Through the ages man has celebrated nature's beauty by decorating with organics…elements found in the environment or made from natural materials. From flower arrangements on end tables to rock gardens, wood carvings, clay vessels, seashell collections and much more, man has brought nature home. Organics are used functionally as well as cosmetically to make rope, string, tiles, dinnerware and clothing.

Over the years scrapbookers have explored ways to incorporate organics into their art. Organic embellishments such as dried flowers and leaves, jute or hemp string, rocks, spanish moss, leather, wood, clay tiles, seeds, feathers, sea glass, raffia, pine needles, wheat straw and twigs bring nature's voice to scrapbook spreads. They reflect and support the theme when placed beside meaningful journaling and outdoor photos. Used in their natural state, or stamped, cut, stained or layered, these gifts from the great outdoors can be used to embellish tags, envelopes, titles, borders, photo mats or as stand-alone page embellishments. Organic embellishments are sold in scrapbook or hobby stores. Pick up your favorites, or take a walk around the block. You're sure to find elements that just beg to be showcased in your album.

Until I Saw the Sea
Frame a photo with sea treasures

Valerie adds an organic element to a seaside photo with a partial border of small seashells nestled inside of a fabric frame. Tear four blue vellum strips; horizontally layer at top and bottom of page. Mount embellished padded fabric frame over photo matted on blue cardstock and torn mulberry paper. Add small seashells inside of frame with glue dots. Write title on vellum tags. Tear hole in one vellum tag; embellish with beaded wire. Print journaling on vellum; crop into tag shape. Cut second tag from blue textured cardstock; punch small square at bottom of tag. Embellish tag with lace and seashell. Tie tags together with thin satin ribbon; mount vellum tag to page and let top tag dangle free.

Valerie Barton

Deep Thoughts
Collage textured elements

Valerie adds texture to collaged elements with jute string woven through meshed paper. Freehand tear tan cardstock; crumple, flatten and brush with brown chalk. Mount over blue background cardstock that has been lightly brushed with sandpaper. Cut black corrugated cardstock into photo corners and decorative strip; tear edges and mount on photos. Attach mesh strip to page with eyelets; weave jute string through mesh. Print journaling on vellum; cut to size and tear edges before layering on page. Die cut title letters from textured cardstock. Stamp remaining title letters on tan paper with brown ink. Freehand cut frame for title word from suede leather; layer over title word and mount on page. Attach silver star brads. Layer small tan paper torn square over brown corrugated cardstock torn into triangle shape and attach large silver eyelet before mounting on page.

Valerie Barton

I like my embellishments to capture the mood of the photos on the page. A spread of a misty and rugged sea coast was a good place to try a new technique that involved ironing folds and creases into background paper before scrunching it. The vellum and pale blues help carry a peaceful feeling.

Trudy Sigurdson

Trudy Sigurdson

Super Scrappin' Getaway

Stitch a netted border

Trudy catches starfish and sand dollars in a stitched coastal netting border. Spray light blue cardstock with water; randomly crease paper and iron fold. Repeat process until creases are evenly distributed throughout. Lightly crumple cardstock; flatten and horizontally tear at bottom. Stitch large and small pieces over a 2" strip of coastal netting to a dark blue cardstock background. Gently curl edges of light blue cardstock with fingers; brush edges with black chalk. Mount starfish and sand dollars along coastal netting border. Tie hemp string into knots at 3" intervals; mount along bottom of page. Mat photos on dark blue cardstock. Print title and journaling on vellum. Tear journaling into 1" strips; insert strips in between jute string loops knotted at 1¼" intervals. Tie vellum journaling block with jute string before mounting on page.

I've Been Working on the Railroad

Accent sticker with natural elements

Small, black crystallized rocks look like a mound of coal atop a locomotive sticker on Kelli's thematic layout. Print title words on tan cardstock; silhouette cut with a craft knife before layering on matted title strips. Trim edges of large photo with corner rounder; double mat and mount railroad track die cut around edges of photo. Attach eyelets at corners of title blocks and upper corners of photo mat. Link together with jute string. Print journaling on tan cardstock; mat and detail with a ¼" strip of red cardstock. Mat smaller photos on tan and red cardstock. Mount a few photos with self-adhesive foam spacers; wrap corners of photos with jute string. Adhere locomotive sticker at bottom of page; mount small black crystallized rocks atop sticker with heavy two-sided tape.

Kelli Noto

I really feel that black-and-white photos allow you to focus more on the faces of your subjects because you don't have the distraction that color generates. I actually shoot in black-and-white about 25 percent of the time. But on other occasions I'll shoot in color or shoot digital pictures and may print them in black-and-white afterwards.

Kelli Noto

Patriot

Antique cardstock with tea stains

Tea-stained paper enhances Diana's sepia-toned photos. Stain cardstock with plain brewed tea applied with an eye dropper; dry. Cut title letters, tag and photo mat from tea-stained cardstock. Mat title letters on navy blue cardstock; silhouette cut. Cut tag; scrape edges with scissor blade. Attach eyelet; tie fibers. Mount fabric tag and sticker to tag. Slice four ½" tan cardstock strips; tear one side of each strip. Chalk torn edges in brown and red. Mount strips around edges of photo; layer photo corners over torn strips. Print journaling onto tea-stained cardstock. Crumple, wet and iron journaling block. Add distressed details by rubbing black and gold chalk over cardstock. Tear and curl edges before mounting under red thread secured to page with copper nailheads.

Diana Graham

Diana Graham

Time

Stamp hugs and kisses on pebbles

Diana stamps a message of love on small rocks collected by her daughter. Layer cropped photos on red mesh cardstock and dark blue rectangles torn around the edges. Cut photo corners from dark blue cardstock; tear edges before mounting on one photo. Freehand cut title letters from red mesh cardstock; mount on clay art tiles. Layer tiles over paper-torn cardstock squares; stitch to page with tan embroidery thread. Mount large copper eyelets on page; hang folded tan and red mesh cardstock over jute string strung through eyelets. Print journaling on tan paper; cut to size and mount inside folded cardstock. Stamp sentiment on copper tag; tie clay lettered tile at one end before layering with dark blue torn cardstock strip. Stamp "X" and "O" on small rocks and "MOM" on background with red ink at bottom of page. Mount rocks on page with liquid adhesive.

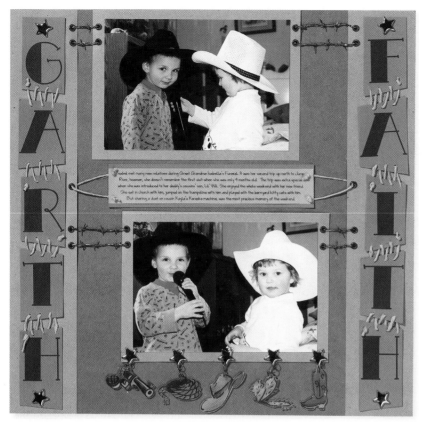

Heidi Schueller

Garth/Faith

Twist "barbed wire" Accents

Heidi adds rustic country elements to her page with "barbed wire" accents. Slice two 2" border strips from tan cardstock. Print title letters onto green cardstock. Cut letters into approximately 1 x 1½" sections. Pierce top and bottom of each section; stitch sections together with hemp string. Mount sections on border strips; attach silver star nailheads. Mat photos on tan cardstock. Attach green eyelets to border strips and photo mats. Craft barbed wire embellishments by twisting small pieces of wire around two strands of wire using needle-nosed pliers. Feed "barbed wire" through eyelets; secure at back of border and photo mat. Print journaling on vellum; cut to size and mat on green cardstock. Secure to page with hemp string looped through green eyelets on border strips. Mount silver star nailheads along lower edge of bottom photo. Attach shrunken plastic designs to nailheads with linked jewelry jump rings.

Gone Fishing

Dangle die-cut fish on a rope border

Heidi shows off the catch of the day with die cut fish layered over a rope border. Print title and journaling on tan cardstock; mount on green cardstock background. Cut green corrugated cardstock to fit inside title letters. Freehand cut trees; add chalk details before mounting at the bottom of the page. Freehand draw fishing net pattern. Cut pattern pieces from cardstock. Crop photos to fit net design. Cut two pieces of rope. Mount on sides of pages. Mount die-cut fish with self-adhesive foam spacers over rope for dimension.

Heidi Schueller

Feed the Birds

Enhance die cuts with spanish moss

Brandi's spread features "tweet" birdhouses embellished with dimensional details. Mat photos on green and blue cardstock. Print title words and journaling on tan cardstock. Cut out title letters; mat on blue, red and green cardstock. Tear around the edges of a few; detail with eyelets and small brads. Mat journaling on green cardstock textured with a crimper. Punch small holes at top of journaling block; tie jute string through holes before "hanging" on page from a small brad. Layer birdhouse die cuts over black and red cardstock so color shows through cut-outs. Punch heart from tan cardstock; mount on red birdhouse. Add spanish moss at top of birdhouses to resemble nests. Mount two birdhouses with self-adhesive foam spacers over strips of jute.

Brandi Ginn

I do take it into consideration, but I'm truthfully not as concerned today about archival issues as I once was because I do such a good job of archiving my negatives. I figure that if a supply—the moss on a page perhaps, or something else—hurts my photos twenty years down the road, then I'll just make prints and replace the damaged ones.

Brandi Ginn

I just love these pictures of Aysha, they really show the various sides of her personality. When I look at the larger photo it reminds me of a Clark's shoes commercial that was on TV in England during the 70's when I was growing up. It had this one little girl that possessed some "diva" like qualities and she said at the end of the commercial "when I grow up I'm going to be a proper little madam!" My family ALWAYS bugged me that that would be me when I'm older... well, I'd like to think it isn't but I do think that it is very fitting for my

MiSS AYSha

Here is a child that I could threaten would have to wear pants instead of a skirt as a punishment! (when she was 2 or 3) Aysha is 10 going on 16 and I'm sure will be the child that I have my battles with during her teenage years. But deep down inside she is just a little girl who wants to be a princess and likes to be hugged and cuddled. I just hope it always stays that way because I will always love my "proper little madam"! Journaling - April 13th 2003. Photos - Beaver Lake Park, October 2001

Trudy Sigurdson

Miss Aysha
Layer organic elements for a border

Trudy layers a variety of elements for an interesting border. Mat mustard-colored textured cardstock on rust cardstock. Tear two 1" strips of rust cardstock for border strips; brush dark brown chalk along torn edges. Attach eyelets at top and bottom of torn paper strip. String metal hearts and stars on raffia before mounting on border strips. Tie hemp string on metal hearts and stars; tie key charm to one heart. Layer dried leaves, vintage stamps and mica tiles on background; mount border strips atop layered design. Secure raffia ends to back of page. Print journaling on transparency; layer over dried leaf, mica tile and stamp. Secure to page with flat eyelets. Wrap and tie twigs with raffia; mount on border strip and journal block. Mat photos on rust cardstock; mount on page.

I have always felt comfortable working with color, but recognize that not everybody feels that way. When determining the colors to use on my pages, I draw from the background elements in photos and take cues from things like the way the sun throws warm gold highlights on hair.

Trudy Sigurdson

Branded by the Effects of Nature

Add rustic appeal with textured fabric

Stamped leather and burlap add rustic charm to Valerie's page. Tear two 3" patterned paper strips; mount horizontally near the bottom of page. Mat two photos on golden yellow cardstock; tie one with hemp before matting. Layer both on patterned paper strips. Craft plastic frame by watermark stamping onto transparency; sprinkle with golden yellow embossing powder and heat set. Tear edges and inside of transparency to create frame and decorative strip. Mount embossed transparency frame to page over large photo with eyelets. Attach burlap strip to bottom of one photo with eyelets. Mount on page; layer with embossed transparency strip. Stamp title letters with brown ink on distressed leather remnant; press brown ink pad around the edges. Cut three tags from patterned paper; tear bottom edges of tags. Print balance of title letters on vellum; tear into strips and layer over torn yellow cardstock strips. Cut small pieces of burlap into top of tag shape; mount atop tag with eyelets. Punch two small holes at bottom corners of leather piece; tie jute through holes connecting title tags together. Print journaling on vellum; tear around edges and layer with torn paper strip and dried leaf. Stamp name on torn piece of patterned paper; layer metal frame attached with eyelets. Layer on page with burlap remnant, leather strip and button.

Valerie Barton

Queen Victoria's Memorial

Create subtle decoration with pressed flowers and leaves

Dried and pressed flowers and leaves enhance Trudy's monochromatic layout. Horizontally layer and mount ivory spring roll strips with tan eyelets on patterned paper. Double mat photos, using crumpled and flattened tan cardstock for the second mat. Stitch matted photos to page; gently curl edges of tan matting with fingers. Print title and date on ivory cardstock; cut title block to size. Mount pressed leaves and flowers on title block; pen border around edge. Mat title block on crumpled and flatted tan cardstock embellished with buttons and hemp string layered on an ivory paper strip. Cut date into tag shape; attach eyelet. Tie tag to decorative square embellished with flowers, leaves, hemp and buttons. Stitch matted title block and decorative square to page.

Trudy Sigurdson

Torrey Miller

Adonis Narcissus Diggs

Add charm with wooden embellishment

A pre-made wooden fence adds simple charm to Torrey's heritage page. Double mat patterned paper with solid colored cardstock. Double mat photo. Cut oval in cropped vellum to highlight subject in photo. Cut oval frame from solid-colored cardstock; layer on vellum. Mount vellum to top of matted photo with gold brads. Mount wooden picket fence along bottom of page. Print journaling on vellum; cut to size and mount on fence.

Diana Hudson

Mother's Day

Highlight dried flowers with pre-made paper frames

Delicate dried daisies encapsulated in memorabilia pockets make a fresh springtime border. Print journaling on textured cardstock background. Cut strip of meshed paper; mount horizontally at bottom of page. Place pressed flowers in memorabilia pockets to keep them from crumbling. Layer pre-made paper frames over encapsulated flower before mounting on page. Mat one photo on dark green textured cardstock. Frame smaller photo with pre-made paper frame. Print title on vellum; cut to size before layering over protected pressed daisy. Mount pre-made frame over vellum title block.

Captured

Add a textured touch with fringed mesh

A solitary photo layered over fringed mesh gives a contemporary look to Diana's layout. Cut a 6 x 12" piece of patterned paper; print title. Print journaling on solid green cardstock. Mount patterned paper with title over solid green cardstock and mat on brown speckled cardstock. Cut a 14" strip of mesh. Wrap around the middle of the page and attach on the back of the page. Mount enlarged photo over mesh strip. String button on green satin cording; tie at ends and mount over mesh and photo.

Diana Graham

Year of the Dress

Build a balsa wood "dressing room"

Heidi designs a "dressing" room to showcase paper dolls of her daughter. Tear a 2" strip of black cardstock and patterned paper; horizontally layer at bottom of page over background patterned paper. Craft "dressing room" from lightweight pieces of balsa wood mounted on patterned vellum and cardstock. Place magnetic sheet behind windows. Mount lightweight hobby hinges to the back of "dressing room" and doors. Paper fold vellum pockets; mount over torn paper strips. Silhouette cut photos; mount on magnetic sheets and crop. (Dolls may sit in windows after page completion). Print title on yellow and journaling on rust cardstocks. Silhouette cut title letters; mat on black cardstock and silhouette again. Paper tear around balance of title; punch flowers from vellum and cardstock and layer. Mount journal blocks behind "dressing room" doors.

Heidi Schueller

Katherine Brooks

Uniquely You

Stamp and emboss a clay tile

Katherine crafts a unique clay title block. Cut a 5" piece of patterned paper; vertically layer over rust cardstock. Layer green gingham ribbon at edge of patterned paper strip; mat background with dark green cardstock. Print journaling on ivory cardstock; cut to size and gently curl right edges with fingers. Ink edges of journaling blocks. Mount on page with small brads at left side of journal blocks. Mat large photo with tan cardstock; wrap bottom with knotted copper wire. Create the clay title tile by first molding polymer clay into a rectangular block. While still malleable, press in title letters and flower stamps. Heat the clay block with an embossing gun; color with metallic rub-on's. Heat again; sprinkle with clear ultra thick embossing enamel and emboss.

Pure Country

Use mesh for textured dimension

Katherine's embossed elements give rustic charm to a country page. Using a craft knife, cut a ¼" frame from brown cardstock; mount over matted mesh background with foam tape. Crumple, flatten and iron patterned paper; mat on brown cardstock. Attach flat eyelets at corners before matting again on layered mesh background. Mat all photos on blue cardstock. Emboss metal tag with ultra thick embossing enamel; while embossing powder is still warm, press in black inked letter stamps. Attach jump ring to tag; string on twine wrapped around matted photos on left page. Emboss paper clip with copper powder; clip photo to background at bottom of page. Cut title letters from corrugated cardstock; emboss with copper powder. Print balance of title and journaling on tan cardstock; cut to size and tear bottom edge. Ink edges of title and journal blocks and mesh scraps. Staple title block to patterned paper. Slice ½" border design in brown cardstock on right page using a craft knife and metal straight-edge ruler. Layer over green mesh and green cardstock with foam tape. Emboss small metal tag in same way as described above; attach tag to mesh with jump ring. Double mat one photo with distressed patterned paper; attach flat eyelets on second mat. Double mat small photos; use embossed corrugated cardstock for second mat. Layer journaling block over sliced blue cardstock strips; attach flat eyelet at lower right corner over mesh scrap.

Katherine Brooks

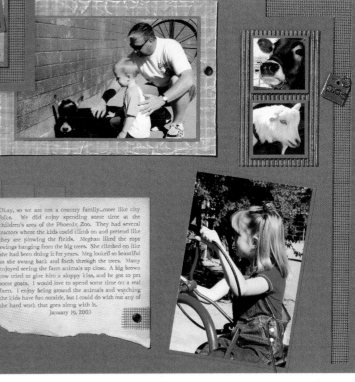

Full of Beans

Craft a shaker box full of beans

Special treasures found in a boy's pockets are packaged in Katherine's homemade shaker box tags. Unwrap tan paper yarn; horizontally mount along bottom of page with silver brads at 2½" increments on olive green cardstock. Mat with dark green cardstock. Single and double mat photos on light and dark green cardstock. Wrap two matted photos with dark green waxy flax. Crimp three 1½" strips of light green cardstock; emboss with green ink and ultra thick embossing enamel. Mount photo over crimped and embossed strips with self-adhesive foam spacers. Print title letters; silhouette cut. Mat large letters on tan cardstock and silhouette again. Print journaling on ivory cardstock; cut to size and brush the edges with brown chalk. Cut tag shape from stamped and crumpled light green cardstock. Punch window in tag with square punch; attach screen to back of window. Punch circles for tag holes; tie with fibers. Sculpt "beans" from polymer clay; bake as directed on packaging. Adhere foam tape on back of tag around edges; before sealing to page, add clay beans.

Katherine Brooks

I knew I wanted to use beans on the page but I didn't have beans in the cupboard—it's just too hot in Arizona to heat up the stove so I seldom cook. I made these beans out of polymer clay, and they look absolutely perfect.

Katherine Brooks

Amigo at the Denver Zoo

Layer a unique textured background

Think outside the box when looking for organic textures to enhance your pages. Brandi's use of a latch-hook rug mesh gives a unique textured background to her zoo spread. Mount latch-hook rug mesh on tan cardstock with sticky dot adhesive. Single and double mat photos on yellow and green cardstock; detail mats with black fine tip pen. Print title letters on green cardstock; silhouette cut. Print journaling on tan cardstock; cut to size and mount.

I first started scrapbooking for my children. Although I still do it for my children I also do it for myself. There's a great sense of accomplishment that comes from preserving our family's history.

Brandi Ginn

Brandi Ginn

Gardening 101

Plant a flowerpot

Heidi plants seeds of knowledge within this flowerpot of pressed flowers and curled wire stems. Print title on ivory cardstock; cut to size, chalk edges and mount vertically over tan cardstock. Punch squares from cardstock in shades of pink and red; mount along edge of title strip. Mat photos on red and pink cardstock; attach eyelets at corners. Frame photos with hemp strung with seed and letter beads. Mat again on cardstock, leaving room for photo captions. Print photo captions on ivory cardstock; brush pink chalk around the edges before mounting on second mat. Freehand cut and layer flowerpot; detail edges with chalk. Laminate pressed flowers; silhouette cut. Punch teardrop shapes for leaves from green cardstock; mat on lighter green cardstock and silhouette cut. Wrap green wire around a pencil to curl; remove and bend to shape. Mount flowerpot, pressed flowers and leaves on page with self-adhesive foam spacers over curled wire.

Heidi Schueller

Holle Wiktorek

Destin, Florida

Scatter sea glass

Holle's warm memories of a seaside vacation come to life with sandy letters and sea glass. Tear two 1¼" strips of tan cardstock; chalk torn edges and press tan ink pad on strips. Horizontally layer over blue cardstock at bottom of page. Freehand cut palm tree trunk from corrugated cardstock and leaves from green cardstock. Crumple and chalk leaves. Place double-sided adhesive sheet on cardstock before die cutting title letters. Cut through both layers; coat with decorative sand. Mount die-cut letters on torn paper strips among mounted sea glass. Double mat photo; mount on background. Cut tags from tan cardstock; stamp sand dollar and family names on tags with brown ink. Stamp sentiments on light green cardstock with brown ink; paper tear and layer on tags. Punch hole at top of tags; layer and mount to page with star brad.

Seeking Shelter

Layer a distressed collage

Diana captures the essence of an imaginative day of military play with rustic layers. Mat one photo on green cardstock; tear edges of matting and rub with black chalk. Roughen edges of photo by scraping with blade of scissors; mat. Crumple, flatten and chalk tan cardstock. Tear distressed paper into thirds; randomly tear holes into cardstock. Layer and mount torn strips with mesh pieces and photos over patterned background paper. Wrap copper wire through mesh and around torn cardstock. Attach eyelets; loop and tie jute through eyelets. Print title word and letters on tan and green cardstock; tear paper and chalk around edges. Wrap title word block with copper wire before mounting on page. Print journaling on green cardstock; tear around edges and add chalk for dimension. Tie small piece of jute at upper right-hand corner; mount journal block on page with self-adhesive foam spacers.

Diana Graham

Valerie Barton

Fishing

Create an accent with handmade paper strips

Valerie uses textured handmade paper to provide interest to a simple layout. Slice a 3" strip of rust cardstock, a 3½" strip of tan cardstock and a 4" strip of brown cardstock. Slice three 1¼ x 2½" rectangles in rust cardstock with a craft knife and straightedge ruler; layer over larger cardstock strips and stitch together. Layer photo with torn edges over torn handmade paper strip before mounting at center of stitched border. Tear two 1" strips of handmade paper; horizontally layer on page about 4" apart. Mat large photos on tan cardstock; layer one over rust torn cardstock strip before matting. Tear edges of small photo; mount on vellum tag. Mount all photos on page. Stamp title word with green ink on bag. Embellish "tag in a bag" with unique items; layer and mount corkboard strip, mesh square, torn paper pieces, swirled paper clip and buttons. Wrap embellished tag with fishing line; mount on page. Journal on tag and tie fibers before sliding into embellished bag. Tie button with jute; mount on torn handmade paper strip.

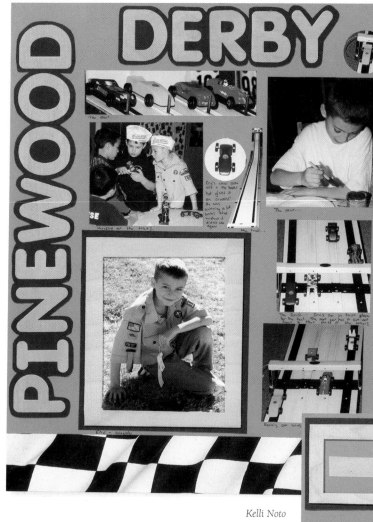

Pinewood Derby

Build interest with wood paper

Kelli documents what it takes to build a car with a border showing creative progression steps. Cut a 2½ x 10¾" piece of wood paper for right-hand page border. Punch five square "windows" in border strip. Mount on red cardstock strip of the same size; mat on black cardstock. Freehand cut visuals from cardstock and wood paper for "windows" showing how to build a handmade car. Attach black eyelets as car wheels in fourth window. Punch scalloped circle from blue cardstock; layer over freehand cut "ribbons" for last window. Slice two 1¾" strips of preprinted photo strip; horizontally mount at bottom of red cardstock background. Die cut title letters from wood paper; mat on black cardstock and silhouette cut around words. Cut two frames from wood paper; mount over matted photos with self-adhesive foam spacers for dimension. Crop and mount balance of photos; write photo captions with black fine-tip pen.

Kelli Noto

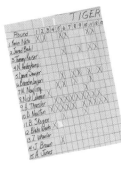

Uninvited Grill Guests

Scatter feathers for a nature accent

Nature inspired Holle's layout documenting the hatching of ten baby birds in her backyard barbecue. Single and double mat photos on light blue, tan and brown cardstock. Print journaling on tan cardstock; cut to size and tear two edges. Double mat on cardstock with torn edges and torn mulberry paper. Cut a few title words from black and blue cardstock; mount on cardstock, cut to size and mat. Adhere letter stickers to matted cardstock strip for one title word. Write the last title word on matted cardstock strip. Freehand draw, cut and papercraft camera, hands and barbecue from cardstock; detail with black and white pens and brush with chalk. Craft nest from cut pieces of paper yarn mounted atop unwrapped paper yarn strips. Cut or punch ovals for eggs; detail with black pen and mount at center of nest. Randomly mount feathers around title and journaling blocks.

Holle Wiktorek

I am strongly into non-event scrapbooking. Events such as Christmas and birthdays come only once a year, but the smaller events are what make up the bulk of our lives. Those are the things that I want to celebrate in my albums. Scrapbooking them allows me to throw myself into the daily blessings.

Holle Wiktorek

Textiles

Early production of fabrics and fibers began around 5,000 B.C. when flax was first spun into a fine linen used for ancient burial shrouds. Other natural fibers, including cotton and wool, were spun into fabrics by the Egyptians several thousand years later, and the Chinese introduced silk as a precious commodity in about 1725 B.C. Until the Industrial Revolution, which brought the invention of the cotton gin and flourishing of factories in the early 19th century, fibers were produced on smaller spinning and weaving looms. Things changed in the late 1890s when manufactured fibers, like rayon, nylon and polyester, came on the textile scene, providing greater comfort, durability and colorfastness.

The immense versatility in color and texture of natural and man-made textiles have made it a choice embellishment for scrapbookers. Ribbon, with its many colors, patterns, textures and widths, can be crafted into dimensional shapes or layered as a simple and elegant design element. Lace, which was a popular fashion embellishment in the 15th century, is now used for photo mats, borders and other scrapbook adornments. Other fabrics can be cut, torn, woven, sewn, layered, embroidered, stuffed, collaged and beaded and tied for unique effects in albums. However you implement textiles into your layouts, you're sure to increase visual appeal by adding a textured touch to your page.

And Tia Makes Three
Add warmth with fringe and fibers

Trudy adds warmth to a rich monochromatic layout with fringed fabric that invites the onlooker to touch the page. Cut two 7 x 11¾" pieces of fabric; mount on textured paper. Stitch around three edges onto dark brown cardstock. Wrap bottom of page with monochromatic fibers; secure to back of page. Mat photos with dark brown cardstock; double mat large photo on mesh before mounting on page. Die cut tags from metallic paper; punch hole and tie fibers. Embellish tags with mesh square and themed buttons. Print title and journaling on transparency; cut to size. Mount journaling blocks on page with small brads. Embellish title and journaling blocks with themed buttons.

Trudy Sigurdson

Letters to My Son

Wrap journaling in charming details

A mother-to-son conversation resounds on this beautiful spread. Mat light green cardstock with olive green cardstock. Cut two 2" strips of mesh; horizontally mat along bottom of pages. Mount knotted hemp string at top edge of mesh strip. Mat photos on olive green cardstock; mount along bottom of page. Attach flat eyelets to background between photos. Tie key charm and Chinese coin with beaded hemp; vertically wrap around large photo. Mount on page with photo corners. Print journaling on putty-colored cardstock; tear edges and brush with chalk. Cut two large tags from olive green cardstock; detail edges with fine-tip black pen. Punch circle; mount at top of tag and attach eyelet. Layer torn journaling blocks on tags and mesh. Wrap beaded jute string around top and bottom of tags. Tie jute at top of tag and around key before mounting on journal block. Stamp title words on putty cardstock; paper tear edges and brush with chalk. Layer paper-torn title words over mesh onto tag (created as described above); wrap title tag with hemp.

Trudy Sigurdson

Sepia-toned photos are beautiful but they can look flat. I love to use them on scrapbook pages but, when doing so, I like to use textiles on the spreads to add dimension and texture that the photos lack.

Trudy Sigurdson

Brandi Ginn

Pumpkin Patch

Embellish preprinted papers with fibers

Brandi adds charm with seasonal dimensional details and fibers. Embellish preprinted paper tags with fibers by slicing the angled end; gently lift and punch a small hole to attach fibers. Cut coordinating patterned paper in shape of tag; tear in half and mount on first and third tag. Embellish with buttons layered over torn cardstock; mount cork scrap. Mat two photos on patterned paper; tear top edge before mounting on page. Tear out the middle of a shaded section; gently curl edges outward. Mount photo behind paper-torn "window." Crop small photos; mount on shaded areas. Mat large right-hand page photo on patterned paper; tear bottom edge. Punch holes at upper corners; tie fibers. Mount on page with self-adhesive foam spacers. Cut large tags from yellow cardstock; detail edges with chalk and pen. Attach eyelet at top of tags over punched leaf shape; tie fibers. Stamp title. Print journaling on yellow cardstock; detail edges with chalk and pen.

Witchie, Witchie

Spin a fibered web

Diana catches the spirit of Halloween with a fiber web. Tear lower right corner of patterned paper; mount over orange cardstock. Punch large circle from orange cardstock; shade edges with purple chalk. Punch small holes in circle; tie sheer black ribbon before layering on black torn cardstock corner. Mat photo on purple paper; tear edges and brush with black chalk. Mount under black torn corner over patterned paper. Craft web from black embroidery thread; mount on lower right page corner. Tuck ends under torn patterned paper edge. Mount buttons, tied with purple and black embroidery thread, along torn pattered paper edge. Cut tag from patterned paper with printed journaling. Attach eyelet and tie fuzzy fiber; mount over crafted web. Layer die-cut spider over embroidery thread strip; mount on page with self-adhesive foam spacers. Write title on torn vellum block. Print journaling on vellum; cut and mount on page. Embellish title and journaling block with seed beads.

Diana Graham

Arizona Fall

Collect fibers in fall colors

Katherine ties together colors of the season with fibers and photos of a colorful Arizona autumn. Tear one edge of gold cardstock; mat on dark brown cardstock for background. Crumple and flatten light brown cardstock; apply metallic rub-ons with cotton swab. Double mat large photo; use textured cardstock for second mat. Punch leaf from thin copper square; emboss and stamp name and date in leaf and square. Tie copper leaf to fibers; wrap around photo mat. Print title on dark gray cardstock; silhouette cut and apply copper metallic rub-ons with fingertips. Double mat letter "O" on light and dark brown distressed cardstock. Slice ¼" strips of rust cardstock; cut into ½" pieces. Mount around "O" to look like a sun. Mat series of three photos on a single cardstock strip; mount at bottom of left page. Double mat photo series on right page; mount the center photo on strip with self-adhesive foam spacers. Print title word and journaling on ivory cardstock; detail edges with black pen and tan chalk. Cut title block to size; mount on page with small brad. Slice a 1" strip of textured cardstock; mount at top of right page. Attach eyelets at each end. Tie fibers to each side of punched copper square; string through eyelets.

Katherine Brooks

I love adding simple detail to my layouts. As for my style...
I love country décor and find that it transfers into my layouts.

Katherine Brooks

A Mother's Pride

Add monochromatic texture with fiber and seashell borders

Subtle, textured details call attention to Trudy's black-and-white seaside photos. Print title, journaling and poem on light blue cardstock; cut to size. Crumple and flatten title; mat on blue cardstock and mount at top of page with small silver brads. Cut poem into small squares to fit inside die-cut vellum envelopes. Attach silver eyelets to poem tags and tie fiber at top. Single and double mat photos. Using a craft knife and straightedge ruler, slice two windows in light blue cardstock larger than the large matted photo and printed journaling block. For left-hand page, lay cardstock with sliced window over darker blue cardstock. Mount fibers and small seashells behind window. Wrap light blue cardstock with fibers before mounting on dark blue cardstock background. Repeat the process for right-hand page journaling block. Stamp descriptive words and location on light blue cardstock; cut to size, crumple and flatten. Mount with small silver brads.

Trudy Sigurdson

Within You I See Myself

Wrap a pretty page in ribbon

A shiny hair ribbon ties up this feminine page while metallic details reflect the shine of a mother's love. Mat blue cardstock with darker blue cardstock. Slice two 5" strips of patterned paper; vertically mount at outside edges of each page. Knot ribbon; vertically mount along edge of patterned paper strip. Single and double mat photos on light green cardstock. Emboss edges of double-matted photos with green ink. Attach eyelets at upper corners of second mat. Print journaling on green cardstock; cut into four journaling blocks. Press edges of journaling blocks on tan stamp pad. Print descriptive words on transparency; cut to size and mount over bottom of large photos with small silver brads. Stamp title letters at bottom of page with black ink. Print date on green cardstock; insert into concho and mount on page.

My daughter is a "pink" girl, but I find it difficult to buy scrapbook papers in the shades of pink that she most often wears. So I often choose to photograph her in black-and-white so that I can select the colors without worrying about matching her outfits. These are also the colors I love best and those that support my page theme.

Katherine Brooks

Katherine Brooks

Trudy Sigurdson

When a Child Is Born

Collage textiles for decorative effect

A collection of sheer, metallic and natural elements are collaged on textured paper tiles for a soft monochromatic layout. Pink crumpled, flattened and ironed cardstock is cut into 3¾" squares and mounted on rose cardstock. Horizontally layer paper lace across top of page. Stitch matted photo secured with photo corners to page over paper lace. Print journaling and date onto pink cardstock. Paper tear pink and white cardstock strips; mount at top of journaling block before stitching on page. Collage skeleton leaves, mica tiles, metal heart, buttons, dried flowers and leaves on page. Wrap bottom of page with tied sheer ribbon; tuck ribbon under edges of paper tiles.

The Perfect Dress

Layer lace for a feminine look

Soft details enhance Holle's story of what it takes to find the perfect wedding dress. Print journaling on patterned vellum; tear edges and mount at upper left corner of mauve cardstock. Die cut title letters from felt and cardstock. Heat emboss cardstock letters with silver embossing powder. Layer title letters over vellum and lace strips; border with sparkled yarn. Stamp title word on pink cardstock; cut into ribbon shape and mount at top of page. Mat two photos together; mount over lace strip. Adhere dimensional stickers around photo.

Holle Wiktorek

Katherine Brooks

You Can't Hide Beautiful

Accent a border with ribbon

Gingham ribbon adds a textured touch to Katherine's feminine borders. Slice four 3" strips of patterned paper; horizontally mount at top and bottom of pages. Mount gingham ribbon over pink ½" torn paper strips at patterned paper's edge; wrap around to back of page and mount. Using craft knife and straightedge ruler, slice two cardstock photo frames, one larger than the other from mauve and green cardstock. Heat emboss mauve cardstock frame with pink metallic embossing powder; press heart stamp at top while still warm. Mount on green cardstock frame; layer over large photo. Mat balance of photos on green cardstock. Print title and journaling on vellum; tear edges of title block. Mount with embossed silver brads over pressed flower. Remove center of metal framed tag; layer over vellum journal block. Heat emboss small tag; stamp with heart while warm. Mount on photo with small silver brad.

Jenna

Stitch a torn fabric background

Sheer fabric softly frames photos of this newborn. Mount photos on pink cardstock background with photo corners. Cut fabric to size of background cardstock; stitch around mounted photos. Cut out center of fabric over photos; gather on two sides and secure with stitched ceramic buttons. Tear two 1½" strips of white textured cardstock; gently curl edges. Vertically mount at outside edges of page. Stitch around entire page ¼" from edges. Wrap fibers on paper-torn borders, securing to back of page. Stamp title on white cardstock with lavender ink; tear edges and gently curl. Stitch around edges at center of page.

Trudy Sigurdson

Textiles ✳ 39

Muriel

Stitch a floral bouquet

Torrey draws inspiration from dress details in a heritage photo with an embroidered silk ribbon bouquet. Using a craft knife and straightedge ruler, slice window $\frac{1}{2}$" smaller than photo into 12 x 12" light green cardstock. Mount photo behind light green cardstock. Slice a slightly larger window into $11\frac{1}{4}$ x $11\frac{1}{4}$" dark green cardstock. Freehand draw floral design on dark green cardstock with pencil. Pierce holes into cardstock before stitching with silk ribbon using a variety of embroidery stitches. Mount stitched cardstock frame over light green cardstock frame. Die cut letters into white cardstock. Rub letters on a watermark stamp pad and dip in gold ultra thick embossing powder. Heat from the underside with embossing gun until melted. Mount at bottom of dark green cardstock.

Torrey Miller

Dian Frybarger

Craft a memory board with fabric and ribbon

Torrey nestles vintage photos on a fabric-covered french memory board. Cut fabric to size of cardstock; mount, securing edges to back of page. Cut pieces of grosgrain ribbon to border and criss-cross on page. Layer ribbon as shown; wrap edges around back of page and secure. Mount small buttons at ribbon intersections. Print title and date on yellow cardstock; trim with decorative scissors and mat. Freehand craft fruit and leaves from colored cardstock to match fabric design; detail with chalk. Mat photos on gray, coral and yellow cardstock trimmed with decorative scissors. Nestle title block and photos under ribbon on page.

Torrey Miller

a pinch of sugar

a dash of spice

mixed with everything nice...

that's what little girls are made of!

Heidi Schueller

A Pinch of Sugar

Stitch designs on vellum tags

Simple designs stitched on vellum tags are a sweet addition to Heidi's page that tells the tale of two girls. Print journaling on tan cardstock. Use printed cardstock as first mat for two double-matted photos. Write balance of title on vellum tags with brown pen. Punch hole at top of vellum tags; string brown ribbon through hole; mount under double-matted photos. Tie brown ribbon into small bows; mount at bottom of vellum title tags. Trace leaf and butterfly design onto vellum tags with pencil. Carefully stitch with tan and brown embroidery thread. Punch small holes in vellum tags; tie together with ivory ribbon.

My pages are original to the core. I may use idea books as a start, but when I'm done, nothing is the same as the idea I looked at.

Heidi Schueller

First-Grader

Tie fibers to a colored slide mount

Katherine twists fibers together to secure a colored slide mount holding the title to her page. Mat green cardstock with burgundy cardstock. Slice a 2" piece of patterned paper; tear bottom edge. Create a second patterned paper by rubbing a brown ink pad over neutral cardstock. Slice a 1½" strip of inked patterned paper; tear bottom edge. Horizontally layer patterned papers together; mount at top of green cardstock. Attach two eyelets ½" from edges of page. Color slide mount with pigment powder and adhesive; detail edges of slide with gold leaf pen. Punch small holes at sides of slide mount; attach eyelets. Print title on vellum; cut to size and mount behind colored slide mount. Tie fibers to eyelets on slide mount; string through eyelets on page. Secure fibers on back of page. Mount photos at page center. Horizontally and vertically mount green ribbon around photos. Attach small brads at ribbon intersections. Print journaling on neutral cardstock; cut to size. Press edges of journaling block onto brown ink pad; mount at bottom of page.

First Grader

I was not ready for this day to come. Really, I was not ready. Meghan had completed kindergarten at a near by Montessori school, but because she missed the public schools age cut off by three months they would not let her go into first grade this year. I kept telling myself that maybe this was for the best. She did do very well in school and was even reading a small amount, but maybe socially she wasn't ready. Then a couple days before school started the elementary school had meet the teacher night. We were all ready to go and meet Meghan's kindergarten teacher when I received a phone call from a friend. She was already at the school and saw that Meghan's name was on the first grade list. We were a little confused but excited. The school did know that I preferred her to go into first grade, but I couldn't believe that they had changed their minds. Sure enough when we arrived at the school she was scheduled to be in Ms. Davis' first grade class. I did talk privately to Ms. Davis and we agreed to see how things whet and if it didn't look like it was working out then we would move her back into kindergarten. So see, I really wasn't ready for my little girl to go into first grade. We spent the next two days scrambling to get her supplies, lunch box, and all of those other necessities for the start of her first day. August 15, 2002

Katherine Brooks

First Grader

Spring
Embellish with embroidered stickers

April showers brought May flowers to Holle's layout with colorful embroidered stickers. Slice a $3\frac{1}{4}$" strip of patterned vellum and a $3\frac{3}{4}$" strip of white cardstock; tear one edge of each strip. Horizontally layer at top of page over teal cardstock. Mount embroidered sticker as title over torn layered strips. Horizontally wrap fibers around page securing at back. Crop small photos into tag shapes. Mat tag-shaped photos on pink cardstock. Mount flower eyelet at top of tags; tie with fibers. Mount photo tags at top of page. Mat cropped photo on patterned paper. Print journaling on white cardstock; cut to size. Mat on pink cardstock with paper-torn edge. Embellish photo and journaling mats with flower embroidery stickers.

Excited about going to a family birthday party, Jayce could not stop smiling! She could hardly wait to see her cousin David and to eat her favorite dessert...cake! She hurried Aunt Holle by opening the truck door all by herself, and she sang children's songs the entire way to meet Honey, her grandmother. Today the spring showers could not make Jayce sad because her family would bring her happiness.

Holle Wiktorek

For me, the highlight of becoming a Memory Makers Master was watching my mom have so much fun with it. When we go to a scrapbook store together she insists on telling everyone. I tell her that no one cares, but she keeps on talking!

Diana Graham

How Sweet It Is
Layer tag with textured details

Diana's memo board holds a tag layered with textured papers and dry embossed die-cut flowers. Diagonally layer yellow ribbon across patterned paper; wrap ends around edges and mount to back of page. Mount stitched buttons at ribbon intersections. Mat photos on solid and patterned paper. Stamp flower photo corners; silhouette cut and mount on one photo. Print title and journaling on vellum; cut to size. Paper tear edges of journaling block; mat on patterned paper and mount on page with fibers and beaded hat pin. Layer title block with mesh, untwisted paper yarn and paper-torn patterned paper on tag. Attach flower eyelet; tie with fibers. Stitch bottom of tag and mount small button. Die cut flowers and leaves from magenta, orange and green paper; dry emboss around the edges. Layer flowers and title tag on page.

Diana Graham

Love...

Illustrate a lasting bond with stitching

Diana uses a common metaphor to reflect a strong bond between friends. Mat two photos on one piece of pink cardstock. Horizontally tear matting under bottom photo. Stitch torn pieces back together with black embroidery thread in a zigzag formation, leaving space between the pieces. Print title and journaling along right side of dark pink cardstock background. Cut a piece of printed vellum into square; mount on page. Pierce holes in vellum with paper piercer to ensure even stitches. Stitch around vellum square with black embroidery thread. Brush pink chalk on journaling to highlight specific words.

I'm not a shy person and my pages are a reflection of my personality. I've tried to work with other styles, but it seems that most often, whatever I create turns out colorful!

Diana Hudson

Diana Hudson

Do Not Peek

Add texture with a sheer element

Sheer mesh fabric tied with colored ribbons becomes a textured border on Valerie's page. Mat two photos on pink and green cardstock. Circle cut large circle from white cardstock. Press edge of circle on watermark stamp pad; heat emboss with silver embossing powder. Circle cut third photo; mat on embossed circle. Attach eyelet at top of embossed circle; tie with fringed fibers. Stamp flower design on vellum; print journaling over stamped design. Cut to size and tear top and bottom edges. Mount on page with colored eyelets. Rub colored chalk on metal-rimmed tags; tie with blue yarn. Mount alphabet beads on tags. Cut large piece of mesh fabric. Mount on left side of page, leaving slack in the fabric. Gather together at center and tie with sheer, colored ribbon. Cut out center of square metal rimmed tags; layer with flower button over mesh fabric scrap. Mount metal frame over blue cardstock scrap; write date at center with blue pen.

Valerie Barton

> *I've been sewing since I was 10, so using fabric on scrapbook pages feels very natural to me. While it doesn't show up distinctly when published, I think fabric looks completely different from paper when you are holding the album in your hand. It adds wonderful texture.*
>
> *Brandi Ginn*

Brandi Ginn; Photos Cummings, Aliso Creek, California

We all went to California for Christmas. And while we were there we had to have family pictures taken at the beach. It had been raining all-day and stopped just long enough for us to take pictures and then started up again. We were really lucky!

By California standards it was cold outside but coming from Colorado we felt lucky being outside without our coats on. Alexa had fun running on the beach and Brinley had fun watching her—she wasn't walking yet.

I was thrilled with how cute so many of the pictures turned out.

Beach Bums

Mat photos with stitched fabric squares

Brandi brings the crisp, clean look of California's relaxed lifestyle to her layout with photos matted on stitched pieces of blue linen fabric. Slice a 3¾" strip of patterned paper; tear one side and mount as a border over light blue patterned paper. Gently curl edges. Cut a 5 x 7" piece of patterned paper; tear two edges before mounting at bottom right corner of right page. Stamp title words on background paper with gold ink and heat emboss. Mat photos on pieces of blue stitched fabric. Stamp seashell designs on white cardstock; detail with colored chalks and silhouette cut. Randomly mount on page, use self-adhesive foam spacers on a few for dimension. Encapsulate seashells under watch crystal; wrap fiber around the edge. Stamp "sand" with blue ink on white cardstock; mount large glass pebble over word on border strip. Print journaling on vellum; cut to size and mount over stamped seashell design. Tie fibers to swirl clips; attach to matted photos and border strip.

Sailing at Lake Granby

Craft thematic embellishments from fabric

Kelli takes inspiration from a day out on the lake with maritime accents crafted from fabric, eyelets and twine. Single and double mat a few photos on red and blue cardstock. Freehand cut photo corners from red cardstock for two photos. Craft sailboat sails from white fabric with stitched edges. Attach gold eyelets; string pieces together with twine. Mount atop freehand cut boat layered under freehand cut waves. Craft life preserver from white fabric cut into circle. Mount rectangles cut from red cardstock and twine over fabric circle. Freehand cut waves from blue cardstock; mount along bottom of second page. Die cut letters from red cardstock. Attach eyelets at left side of letters; stitch with frayed twine. Embellish first letter of title word by layering on stitched fabric and cardstock detailed with eyelets and twine.

I'm not a seamstress, in fact I can't sew at all. So, when I use fabric on my pages I need to look for shortcuts. For example, I'll cut material from a piece of clothing or maybe an old ironing board cover in a way that allows me to utilize an edge that has already been stitched. Then I completely cover the material with adhesive to prevent other edges from unraveling.

Kelli Noto

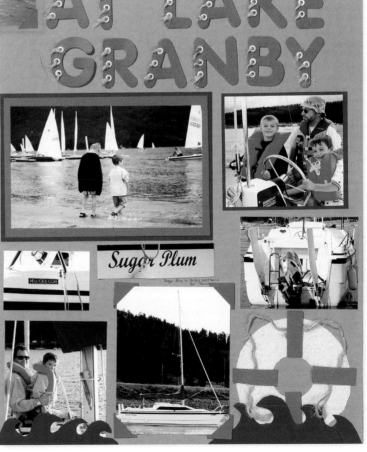

Kelli Noto

Textiles ✦ 45

Zoo Crew
Hide journaling under tied tags

Heidi's page hides journaling under buttoned tags tied together with embroidery thread. Slice ¾" and 1" strips of brown and golden yellow cardstock; tear one edge. Horizontally layer at top of page over rust cardstock background. Cut title letters; mat two times on brown and black cardstock and silhouette cut. Punch a small hole at top of each letter and in layered torn paper strip. Dangle title letters with small wire pieces curved into "S" shape through small punched holes. Double mat smaller photos on freehand cut tag shapes; score right side of tag ¼" from ends. Apply strong adhesive at scored edge of tags only so tags can lift to reveal journaling; mount on page. Mount buttons stitched with embroidery thread on tag; tie a 2½" piece of embroidery thread to buttons. Mount stitched buttons on page to the left of buttoned tag. Print journaling on cardstock; cut to size and mount under tags. Wrap 2½" piece of embroidery thread around button stitched to page to secure. Mat large photo on golden yellow cardstock; apply foam tape adhesive along three edges of photo mat. Mat again on blue cardstock. Print journaling; cut to size to fit inside of space between mattings. Stitch tied button to 1 x 2" strip of cardstock; mount strip behind journaling block with strong adhesive. Slide buttoned journaling block into space between mattings. Tie small buttons with embroidery thread; mount as a border on right side of page.

Heidi Schueller

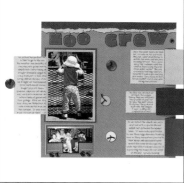

Funny Face
String fringed fibers through eyelets

Colorfully fringed fibers strung across Valerie's photos add an artistic and textured element to her layout. Tear a 4½" strip of mustard cardstock; mount vertically on yellow cardstock as a border. Gently roll edges with fingers. Mat photos on purple cardstock; mount on page. Stamp title words with blue and purple inks. Stamp letters and shape on small yellow cardstock strip; mount metal frame atop strip. Print journaling on golden yellow cardstock lightly stamped with square design. Tear all edges; mount on border. Attach eyelets on border and background cardstock. String fringed fibers through eyelets; secure at back of page. Mount purple buttons on page and border strip. Mount small golden yellow punched squares a bottom right corner.

Valerie Barton

Busy Bee

Stitch the whimsical flight of a busy bee

Heidi photojournals the happenings of her favorite busy bee with colorful clip art and stitched flight lines. Double mat photos on solid cardstock and patterned paper; mount on black cardstock background. Print title words and clip art; mat on yellow cardstock and silhouette cut around shapes and words. Print journaling on yellow cardstock; cut to size and mount alongside photos as shown. Pierce holes in cardstock with paper piercer; stitch flight lines with white embroidery thread.

I love stitching, in fact I'm teaching a class for scrapbookers who want to learn how to sew on their pages. I've enjoyed mixing mediums in my art ever since I was encouraged to do so when I attended the University. Mixing mediums adds dimension and interest.

Heidi Schueller

Heidi Schueller

Memphis

Detail border with sheer ribbon

Sheer ribbon strung through eyelets gives a delicate accent to Valerie's journaling and photos. Mat three photos on green cardstock; mount on patterned paper background. Mat one photo over torn vellum strip before matting on green cardstock. Tie sheer green ribbon at bottom of matted photo. Mat two landscape photos together to look like one panoramic photo on one large piece of green cardstock. Print title and journaling on vellum. Paper tear edges; mount on green cardstock. Attach silver eyelets at top and bottom of journaling block as well as on cardstock border with photos. String sheer green ribbon through eyelets; tie.

Valerie Barton

How much embellishing is enough? I generally take my cue from the photos. When they are streamlined and elements in the pictures are more linear, I tend to make my embellishments look the same. Here, a few strips of ribbon was enough to carry the theme and feel of the layout.

Valerie Barton

*Is more than
I could have
ever hoped for.
I look into your smiling faces and
I see my joy! I never dreamed
motherhood would be so rewarding!*

Valerie Barton

Being Your Mom

Dangle charms on fibers

Valerie's "charm-ing" photo mat dangles seashell charms tied to textured fibers. Slice three 2½" strips from two colors of green cardstock and green vellum. Paper tear one edge; vertically layer and mount at left side of page. Attach silver brad at top and bottom of layered border; vertically wrap fibers around brads. Double mat photo; tear second matting along bottom edge. Wrap fibers along bottom of second mat; tie silver seashell charms to fibers with thread. Print journaling on vellum; paper tear along top and bottom edges. Mount to page under matted photo and over torn vellum strips with silver eyelets. Print title; silhouette cut with craft knife. Cut tag from green cardstock. Attach eyelet; tie with fibers. Embellish tag with torn paper strip and die-cut seagull.

The Smile on Your Face

Embellish with buttons and lace

Valerie adds a feminine touch to patterned paper segments with dainty embellishments. Double mat photo on peach and tan cardstock; tear the top edge of peach mat. Brush torn edge with tan chalk. Wrap satin fiber around photo; tie together with button. Print title words on peach cardstock; mount 12 x 12" embossed vellum over peach cardstock. Using a craft knife, carefully slice a diagonal strip into embossed vellum; slide double matted photo into strip and adhere. Print title word on peach cardstock; silhouette cut. Paper tear a 5½ x 7½" piece of peach cardstock; brush tan chalk around torn edges. Using a craft knife and straightedge ruler, slice square and rectangular windows into cardstock. Mount vellum strip and photo behind cut windows; journal on vellum strip with peach gel pen. Tie fibers to buttons; mount under rectangular window. Layer torn cardstock with windows over vellum strip before matting on tan cardstock. Tie horizontally and vertically with lace and fibers. Cut two squares from patterned paper; mat one on torn cardstock square brushed with rose chalk and double mat the other. Slice a 1" strip from patterned paper; mat on tan cardstock. Stitch buttons to matted strip. Horizontally mount at bottom of page over lace strip.

Valerie Barton

Diana Hudson

I love heritage scrapbooking. I enjoy documenting previous generations for future generations.

Diana Hudson

Dressing Alike

Sew up fond memories

Diana documents her mother's love of sewing with machine-stitched journaling tags and photo mats. Print title onto lavender cardstock. Horizontally stitch a 7½" piece of vellum to patterned paper and mount at the center of the lavender cardstock. Mat lavender cardstock on green cardstock for background. Double mat one photo on purple solid and green patterned papers. Stitch buttons to purple patterned paper strip; mount at top of first matting. Mat photo on folded purple patterned paper; stitch around edges. Tie two photos together with sheer purple ribbon; mount stitched button where photos meet. Print journaling onto purple paper and vellum. Cut large journaling into tag shape. Mat on purple patterned paper; stitch around edges. Attach eyelet; tie fibers. Embellish with stitched buttons at lower right corner. Cut journaling on vellum to size; layer over purple patterned paper with sheer ribbon strips stitched around the edges. Attach vellum to ribbon-trimmed paper with beaded hat pin. Embellish with stitched buttons at lower right corner.

Cut small tag from purple patterned paper; mat on solid purple paper. Stitch around edges and attach eyelet. Tie sheer ribbon to tag; loop over button on journaling block as shown. Cut journaling for small tag to size; layer on tag under dimensional heart sticker.

Fringies

Stitch dimensional flowers

Stuffed and stitched flowers reflect the snugly comfort of a treasured blanket. Divide background into four quadrants; cut colored cardstock to fit quadrants and mount together on the back. Print title words on paper; trace onto 12 x 12" vellum with purple pen. Mount vellum over color-blocked background. Print large title word on vellum; color with brush pens. Stitch around edges of letters with purple embroidery thread; silhouette cut leaving a small border around stitched edge. Mount at top of page with self-adhesive foam spacers. Lightly pencil flowers, stems and leaves on vellum. Cut flowers out of vellum-layered background. Pierce along penciled design to ensure even stitches. Stitch layers together with purple embroidery thread along design lines. Mount gingham fabric behind cut-out flowers over fiber fill for dimensional flowers. Triple mat photo; color block third mat with two colors of cardstock. Attach beaded ribbon at the bottom of third mat. Mount embellished and matted photo at center with self-adhesive foam spacers.

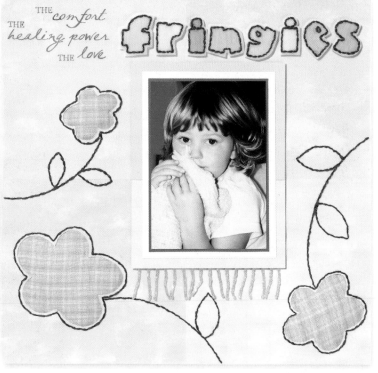

Heidi Schueller

To Dance the Dream

Create fantasy with fringed fibers and embossed snowflakes

Torrey creates a sparkling winter fantasy with large and small snowflakes stamped and silhouette cut into unique designs. Stamp background with snowflake design using watermark stamp. Apply clear embossing powder and heat. Stamp more snowflake patterns and dust with pigment powders. Stamp snowflake designs on vellum. Heat emboss two snowflakes with lavender embossing powder and another with silver embossing powder; silhouette cut. Add sparkling details to another with glitter glue. Print title word on paper; trace onto vellum using watermark pen. Heat emboss with purple embossing powder. Silhouette cut around letters; layer on page over fringed fibers mounted on background. Write smaller title words on vellum with watermark pen; heat emboss with silver embossing powder. Cut to size and mount on page. Double mat largest photo; use torn mulberry paper for second matting. Mat remaining photos on white cardstock. Print journaling on vellum; tear edges and mount between photos.

Since I don't have my own kids, I love scrapping my "adopted" kids...my nephews and my best friend's daughter. I also love to scrap my artistic photos of "stuff"...scenery, textures...stuff...

Torrey Miller

Torrey Miller

frolicking

Malibu, California ~ 2002

Let a joy keep you. Reach out your
hands and take it when it runs by
~Carl Sandburg

Baubles

Humans dating back to the Neanderthal have adorned their bodies and clothing with small objects such as animal bones and teeth, seashells and colorful stones. In the ancient world, beads were viewed as status symbols and were used for bartering in international trade. Stones, bone and other adornments were worn to ward off bad spirits and "lucky charms" dangled on bracelets and necklaces. In the early 20th century the popularity of decorative fashion jewelry boomed. Small lockets, trinkets, glass beads and family crests hung on bracelets and necklaces of the masses.

Flash forward to the art of scrapbooking, where baubles, trinkets and other unique embellishments are helping tell the story behind the photos and are adding their special brand of visual appeal. A large selection of baubles is available at craft stores. But other embellishments such as jewels, beads, buttons, ceramic tiles, charms, glass pebbles, lockets and old jewelry can be found everywhere from fabric stores to garage sales and dusty attics. Use baubles to embellish photo frames, string them to create borders, decorate photos, use them in a collage or in one of the other creative ways you'll find in this chapter.

Diana Graham

The Dance of the Leaves

Detail title with stitched buttons

Stitched buttons, in shades of orange and green, add a homespun touch to Diana's page. Tear edges of mustard paper; mat on orange cardstock with eyelets for background. Horizontally mount panoramic photo as border at top of left page. Print title words on vellum; cut to size. Attach eyelets at title block corners; tie together with fibers and mount on photo border. Mount stitched buttons on title blocks as shown. Single and double mat photos. Die cut frame from vellum; mount over photo on right page. Attach eyelets at corners; string fibers through eyelets and tie. Print journaling on tags; tie fibers and embellish with stitched buttons. Scrape edges of tags with scissors blade; add dimension to edges and around journaling with chalk.

Holle Wiktorek

Best Friends

Add decorative jewels and beads

There are many reasons Holle's mom is her best friend and they are clear in this loving page. Slice a 2" strip of blue cardstock; tear one edge and vertically mount at left side of page. Die cut hearts from red cardstock and title letters from cork. Embellish hearts with tinsel, beaded wire, glitter glue and fibers. Layer embellished hearts with letters on border strip with self-adhesive foam spacers. Paper tear tan and blue cardstock pieces; collage on page. Mount torn tan cardstock piece at upper right corner over tinsel shreds. Die cut title letters from red cardstock; mount on torn cardstock with small mesh scrap. Die cut frame from red cardstock; embellish with glitter glue, mesh scrap, fiber and swirl clip before mounting over photo. Circle cut two photos; mount on die-cut red cardstock circles. Attach blue fiber at back of photo circles; "hang" from flower brad attached to page. Print journaling on mulberry paper; tear edges and mat on red cardstock with torn and curled edges. Die cut wavy frame from red cardstock; embellish corners with blue jewels before matting on corrugated cardstock.

Joy in Blytheville

Add a touch of glitter to punched shapes

Holle decorates holiday memories with punched holly leaves in a variety of textures and shine. Use large letter stickers to create "Joy" title; embellish with ribbon and punched holly leaves. Mount letter stickers on black cardstock trimmed with gold glitter glue. Die cut small title letters from gold cardstock; mount along bottom of title block. Mat oval cut photo on green cardstock oval. Attach metal holly leaves with red eyelets above oval photo. Mat photos on green cardstock; apply gold glitter glue around edges of green matting. Layer matted photos on brown suede paper detailed with gold glitter glue dots. Adhere dimensional wreath sticker at bottom of suede paper between photos. On right page, mat photos on green cardstock. Craft a layered embellishment with punched oak and holly leaves. Mount photo at bottom of right page. Frame photo with punched holly leaves layered over punched oak leaves detailed with gold glitter glue. Mount small red beads at stems of holly leaves to look like berries. Print journaling on tan cardstock; cut to size and mat on green cardstock. Embellish with holly leaves punched from gold cardstock and tied together with red ribbon.

My favorite person to scrapbook is my husband. He makes me happy, and he has shown me things I could never have experienced. Although I scrapbook many events like birthdays, holidays, vacations and seasons, my favorite event to scrapbook is our anniversary.

Holle Wiktorek

Thomas and I stopped by his parents' house in Blytheville on the way to our last adventure before he left the country. We surprised Dad and Ma Cel with a new computer, monitor, and internet service. They surprised us with two accessories to our Snow Village collection: Hershey truck and moving van/movers figures. These were perfect because I love chocolate, and we have lived in three houses within the past year. They also allowed me to choose two new outfits at The New York Store as my Christmas gift. We enjoyed Dad's famous chicken wraps for dinner and a trip to the Dixie Pig during our visit.

Holle Wiktorek

Alex at Beckwith Park
July 1st 2001

love
dream
cherish

Trudy Sigurdson

My Little Man
Stitch a button border

Layers of torn paper are stitched together and secured with buttons to create a soft, textured background for Trudy's black-and-white photos. Tear eight 1½" strips of light blue paper; horizontally mount on light blue background matted with ivory cardstock. Machine stitch around three edges of page. Punch squares from blue paper; mount along outside edges of page at 2½" increments and machine stitch around square. Stitch buttons over squares to complete border. Mat photos on ivory cardstock; mount on page. Print title and journaling on transparencies; cut to size and mount in between torn strips on page. Embellish title and journaling blocks with stitched buttons. Print descriptive words on vellum. Cut vellum and white and blue cardstock into tag shapes. Layer printed vellum over diagonally torn blue cardstock layered on white tag. Stitch around edges of tag. Mount eyelet over punched square; tie fibers. Mount die-cut star to tag; embellish with button threaded with silver wire. Mount tags on page with self-adhesive foam spacers.

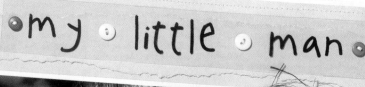

•my • little • man

joy
hope
wonder

friendship

braids

Friendship Braids

Dangle beads from braided embroidery thread

Diana re-creates her daughter's favorite hair embellishment as the perfect accent to dangle from a large slide frame. Print title and journaling on blue background cardstock. Mat photos on patterned paper. Trace slide frame onto patterned paper; cut out shape and mount on top of slide frame. Braid four colors of embroidery thread large enough to wrap around slide; leave ends long to dangle beads from. Add beads at loose ends and knot.

Michelle
Sydney
Rachel

I like to use large photos. I am photo-driven and think nothing should take away from the photos. When you enlarge a great photo it draws your eye and automatically takes center stage.

Diana Hudson

As I look back, I realize now that this was a defining moment in the friendship of these six-year-old girls. As constant companions for over two years, I had the pleasure of watching their friendship grow. On this day as they sat together having their hair braided alike, it occurred to me how intertwined their lives had become. The braiding was uncomfortable, yet they were determined to get through it together.

Diana Hudson

Light of My Life

Embellish tags with beaded wire

Valerie adds color and texture to hanging metal-rimmed vellum tags with beaded wire. Cut teal cardstock into a 7¾" square; tear two edges and mount on patterned paper background. Die cut title letters from teal cardstock; mount on page above torn cardstock square. Print balance of title words and journaling on vellum; tear into strips. Tear seven more strips of vellum; chalk torn edges with pastel colors. Layer title vellum strip over die cut title letters. Weave together printed and plain vellum strips over torn teal cardstock square in an under/over fashion. Slide cropped photo under a few vellum strips to secure. Attach eyelet at lower right corner of second photo; mount at an angle next to title words. Tear a hole from center of vellum and metal tag; wrap tag with beaded wire and punch hole at top of tag through remaining vellum. String fiber through small hole and and attach through eyelet on photo. Embellish other vellum and metal tag with beaded wire bent into "K" shape. Punch hole in vellum; attach fiber through hole and loop around vellum strip. Complete page by wrapping fibers around top of page; secure ends at back of page.

Valerie Barton

Layout design comes fairly easily for me. I find journaling more difficult. I keep a notebook close by to sketch ideas and I've started to write little excerpts in it also. It helps me to write a little and come back a day or two later and write some more.

Valerie Barton

Holle Wiktorek

Flowers

Embellish patterned paper with beads

Holle adds sparkling gold beads to flowers silhouette cut from patterned paper. Slice a 3½" strip of blue patterned paper; tear one edge and horizontally mount over pink patterned paper background. Silhouette cut flowers from patterned paper. Embellish center of flowers with gold beads. Mat photos on green patterned paper. Silhouette cut green leaves from patterned paper; embellish leaves with glitter glue. Mount leaves with self-adhesive foam spacers at bottom of matted photos. Print journaling on patterned vellum and embossed cardstock; cut to size and tear edges. Mount vellum journaling block on gold textured paper with small brads. Cut title letters from green cardstock using letter template.

A Treasured Time
Display heart-shaped trinkets

Diana stitches together a pocket full of treasures. Stamp words on ivory cardstock with pink ink. Cut vellum to fit on top of ivory background; tear top of vellum to form pocket before stitching three sides to page. Mount photos on ivory and pink cardstock. Texture edges of matting by scraping with scissors blade. Stamp photo corners; silhouette cut and mount at two corners of one matted photo. Mount eyelet at the top and slightly off-center of one photo; tie sheer ribbon through eyelet. Mount one photo behind vellum pocket; mount others atop vellum. Mount one small photo behind silver frame. Tear stamped heart; crumple and shade with pink and tan chalk. Mount silver letter over stamped word. String sequins on embroidery thread; mount under stamped word. Stitch heart button to stamped heart with pink embroidery thread. Stamp title on torn ivory cardstock strip; chalk edges. Layer over large patterned heart tag with dangling charms tied with fibers. Print journaling on ivory cardstock; tear edges and chalk. Mat on pink paper with torn edges. Stuff a small chalked envelope with a silver heart charm, vellum and patterned paper heart. Tie silver heart charm with beaded embroidery thread. Punch heart from ivory cardstock; ink around edges and heat emboss with ultra thick embossing enamel. Gently bend and crack when cooled to give the look of antiqued broken glass. Layer at bottom right corner under photo and mount.

Diana Graham

You
Shape title letters with baubles

It's all about "her," on this bright page on which beaded wire, buttons and sequins are shaped into title letters. String fibers at top and bottom of green cardstock background; wrap around edges and secure to back of page. Mat photo on blue cardstock. Cut six ½" slices at top of mat; weave torn patterned vellum strip through slices. Embellish with beads on matting. Print journaling on plain and patterned vellum. Paper tear around specific words; mount torn pieces on vellum with journaling. Tear edges of vellum title block; layer over torn patterned vellum strip on top of blue cardstock. Mount dimensional hearts on square metal-rimmed tags before layering on patterned vellum. Attach small brad at right edge of vellum title block. Heat emboss two or three layers of copper ultra thick embossing enamel on precut mini-mat; stamp flower design with black ink in last layer while still warm.

Valerie Barton

Torrey Miller

Bubbles

Create iridescent bubbles

Torrey captures unburstable bubbles on her page by mounting watch crystals over small circles of patterned vellum. Mount pieces of patterned vellum over lavender cardstock before mounting on page. Cut squares of colored cardstock into various sizes; layer over a purple cardstock background. Mat photos on white cardstock. Cut circles from patterned vellum to fit under watch crystals; randomly mount vellum under watch crystals on page as shown. Use a template to create title letters from blue and lavender cardstock. Mount one letter with self-adhesive foam spacers for dimensional interest. Mount bubble blower die cut; add details with black pen. Mount watch crystal atop die cut.

Bubbly, Sudsily

Craft dimensional bubbles

Heidi creates her own sparkling bubbles with computer-generated art coated with clear micro beads. Horizontally and vertically mat photos on vellum with torn edges. Attach six eyelets to vellum between photos. String beaded wire through eyelets; wrap ends of wire into swirls and bend over vellum to secure. Mount embellished photo mats on blue patterned paper background. Cut title letters from purple cardstock using lettering template. Mat on silver metallic cardstock; silhouette cut. Horizontally and vertically mount under torn vellum strips attached to page with eyelets. Silhouette cut computer-generated bubbles; mount clear micro beads with two sided adhesive tape. Randomly mount beaded bubbles on page. String clear beads on wire; pierce small holes into patterned paper background and attach.

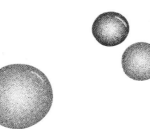

Micro beads are messy to use so if you don't like working with messy stuff, you're going to find them a challenge. Working with micro beads is a bit like adding sprinkles to a sugar cookie. But unlike sprinkles, beads aren't sticky, don't dye your fingers and clean up easily!

Heidi Schueller

Heidi Schueller

Diana Graham

You Make My Heart Leap!

Capture frogs in a shaker box

Diana captures small ceramic amphibians in a tag-shaped shaker box. Mat 4¼" patterned paper strip on white cardstock; vertically mount on patterned paper background with eyelets. Single and double mat photos on yellow, white and green cardstock. Silhouette cut preprinted die cuts; embellish hearts with buttons. Mount title block, heart and frog die cuts with self-adhesive foam spacers. Print journaling on transparency; cut to size and mount under title block. Cut two tags from white cardstock for shaker box; detail edges with green pen and green and yellow chalk. Punch "window" in one tag; mount piece of transparency behind punched window. Mount die cut heart to top of tag with eyelet; embellish with small buttons. Adhere two layers of foam tape on back of embellished tag around edges. Mount frogs to plain tag making sure they will show through window of embellished tag when mounted together. Seal shaker box. Mount eyelet to patterned paper strip; string embroidery threads through eyelets on page and tag. String letter beads on embroidery thread; mount to page through eyelets attached to background between photos.

Kids

Add realistic details with pre-made embellishments

Dragonflies land among a collection of real twigs and hand-crafted leaves and grass. Mat green patterned paper with dark green cardstock. Mount large strip and small square of mesh over patterned paper. Mat photos on ivory cardstock and layer on page over mesh. Print journaling on vellum; tear around edges and mount at bottom right corner of page. Cut title letters from light green cardstock; mat and silhouette cut. Freehand cut leaves and grass from green cardstock. Lightly score along leaf and grass vein lines, bend gently. Mount on page with self-adhesive foam spacers among real twigs and pre-made dimensional dragonflies.

Torrey Miller

Kaitlyn, your smile
is like sunshine...
it warms my
HEART
just to catch a
glimpse of it!
There is nothing
else that can
BRIGHTEN
my day
in the same way.

May 95

You Are My Sunshine

Dangle beaded tags

A collection of seed beads in shades of yellow are adhered to dangling metal-rimmed vellum tags as a visually interesting border embellishment. Slice a 2½" strip of yellow cardstock; crumple and flatten for a textured look. Paper tear one edge; attach eyelets before mounting at top of blue cardstock as a border. Cut tags from green cardstock using template; stamp leaves and title before embellishing with buttons. Print journaling on ivory cardstock; cut to size and mount over green vellum strip with one torn edge. Punch hole through vellum metal-rimmed tag; mount beads with liquid adhesive. String sheer ribbon through hole and tie to eyelet on border. Freehand cut leaves from vellum; emboss line down leaves and gently curl edges together for dimension. Mount at center of pages as shown. Tear yellow mulberry paper into petal shapes; mount together to make a flower. Using a craft knife, slice an ultra thin strip of yellow cardstock; mount as flower's stamen. Double mat photos on blue and yellow cardstock; detail second mat of one photo with beads.

I started scrapbooking to keep a record of my children's events from school. It soon became a creative outlet for me personally. Now I use it as therapy. If I'm having a bad day all I have to do is work on my pages and the problems don't seem as impending doom.

Valerie Barton

Valerie Barton

Making a Splash

Add a sparkling splash of color

Trudy's striking choice of colors is enhanced with glittered geometric designs layered on a black background. Slice three 1¾" wide strips of black cardstock; mat on teal cardstock. Mount at bottom of two pages as a border and at the center of third page. Craft sparkling geometric embellishment from layered punched shapes: punch 31 small squares from colored cardstock. Adhere blue, silver and teal glitter to white cardstock with double-sided adhesive. Punch 31 small circles from glittered cardstock; mount glittered circles on small punched squares. Punch four large circles from blue glittered cardstock; mount on large teal punched squares. Mount large and small squares on border strips as shown; mount large squares over black tinsel for extra pizazz. Print journaling on speckled vellum; cut to size and double mat. Embellish top of journaling block with two small and one large punched squares with glittered circles layered over tinsel as shown. Mount photos on page. Print title words on cardstock; silhouette cut and embellish with glitter. Mount on double-matted speckled vellum. Embellish title block with geometric designs.

Trudy Sigurdson

Jewel of the Pool

Accent elements with jewels

Diana showcases her little mermaid with a paper-piecing kit embellished with sparkling jewels. Assemble paper-piecing kit into mermaid; embellish crown with jewels and mount at bottom of page over patterned paper. Mat one photo on vellum; freehand cut edges in wavy shape and embellish with jewel. Cut title letters from blue cardstock; mount on page and embellish with jewels. Mount cropped photos on right page. Punch circles from blue patterned paper to fit inside metal-rimmed tags. Adhere sticker letters on circle tag; mount in between large title words. Attach eyelet to second tag; tie with ribbon. Make a shaker box out of a metal-rimmed tag by first cutting out the white center. Cut two clear circles from transparency; mount one to back of metal rim. Use two circle punches, one larger than the other, to make a circle frame out of foam. Mount foam frame to back of transparency; fill with beads and mount second transparency to back of foam frame. Finally, mount shaker tag to page with clear adhesive. Print journaling on vellum; cut to size and mount on page. Embellish with jewels at corners.

Diana Hudson

I'm not a trendy kind of woman. I tend to dress in khakis and white shirts. The most "out there" I get is to add a splash of red or blue. I think that monochromatic color schemes more closely reflect my personal style.

Diana Hudson

Moo La La

Feature jazzy and jeweled die cuts

Trudy gives her page Las Vegas shine with glittered die cuts and sparkling jewels. Tear eight 2" strips of black cardstock. Lightly rub torn edges with liquid adhesive before dipping in black glitter. Brush off excess glitter; horizontally mount on black cardstock background. Mount two torn strips at top of page with self-adhesive foam spacers for a dimensional title block. Print title letters on black cardstock; silhouette cut letters. Lightly spray letters with spray adhesive; coat with lavender glitter. Mount title on torn cardstock strip at top of page. Single and double mat photos; mount on page. Print journaling on blue vellum; cut to size and layer on white cardstock before mounting on page. Die cut flowers from colored cardstock; spray with adhesive and coat with glitter. Mount star jewels on glittered flowers before layering on page. Randomly mount jewels on page as shown.

Trudy Sigurdson

A black background is a wonderful backdrop for brightly colored photos. It also allows jewels and glitter to shine vibrantly. It doesn't work for all spreads, but certainly is the perfect canvas to show off something like the glitz of Las Vegas.

Trudy Sigurdson

First Day of School

String beads on wire

Thin wire, sparsely strung with delicate beads, adds an elegant touch to Trudy's page. Slice a 7" strip of lavender cardstock; vertically mount over purple cardstock for background. Mat photos on white cardstock; mount on page as shown. Print title on white cardstock; cut to size and add pen detail around edges. Color empty spaces in title letters with pencil crayons. Mount title block over lavender cardstock strip. Slice 1" strips of patterned vellum; layer and mount at top of page and on white cardstock strip. Mount button tied with fibers atop layered vellum strips. Stamp name on title block. Punch small hole at top of vellum tag; tie with string and "hang" from vellum strip over stamped name. Embellish title block with buttons and silver star. Stamp journaling at bottom of page. String wire with beads. Lay beaded wire on page; pierce small holes in cardstock at one end. Feed wire through hole and bend ends toward page to secure; wrap other wire end around edge of page and secure with tape.

Trudy Sigurdson

Winter

Shake up seasonal fun

Diana frames title and journaling blocks with sparkling snow-filled windows. Mount 11½ x 11½" piece of patterned vellum paper over white cardstock of the same size; mat on purple cardstock. Attach eyelets at corners. Mount photos on purple cardstock. Create title and journal shaker boxes: Print title and journaling on vellum; cut to size. Cut purple paper, patterned vellum and transparency to size of title and journal blocks. Tear out window at center of purple paper; mount transparency to back of torn window. Adhere foam tape to back of top layer; mount to patterned vellum, making sure to fill with shaved ice before sealing. Embellish outsides of shaker boxes with beads and punched snowflakes layered with jewels. Cut two tags from stamped cardstock. Slice window in one tag; mount transparency behind window. Rub edges of tag onto blue ink pad; attach eyelet to tag and tie fibers. Adhere double-sided foam tape around edges of window on back of tag; fill with punched snowflakes and beads before sealing. Write date on small tag; tie with fiber and hang from punched and embellished snowflake.

Diana Graham

Sweet n' Sour

Mount real dimensional embellishments

Torrey's thematic page offers good fortune with real Chinese coins and chopsticks layered amongst a die-cut fortune cookie. Stamp blue cardstock with Chinese lettering; mat stamped cardstock with dark blue cardstock. Tear a 1" strip of dark blue cardstock; horizontally mount at top of page with self-adhesive foam spacers. Heat emboss cardstock with copper embossing powder; freehand cut triangles to shape into title letters. Mount title letters on torn cardstock strip at top of page. Tear a 2½" strip of pink paper; horizontally mount over background near the bottom of the page. Tear a 1" strip of dark blue cardstock; layer over pink torn paper strip. Mat photos on white cardstock; mount atop torn cardstock strips. String fibers with Chinese coins; mount over torn pink paper strip securing ends at back of page. Print "fortune" journaling on white cardstock; cut to size. Mount die-cut fortune cookie and chopsticks on page with self-adhesive foam spacers and glue dots. Slide fortune into fortune cookie.

Torrey Miller

Torrey Miller

Fish

Embellish fish tales with colorful lures

Colorful fishing lures embellish special memories of a dedicated fisherman. Rub black, yellow and red cardstock over texture plates for a subtle dimensional look. Slice a 2½" strip of yellow and red textured cardstock; paper tear one edge before vertically mounting at sides of page. Gently curl edges with fingers. Cut title letters using template from red textured paper; paper tear around edges of letters. Mount atop torn yellow cardstock border with self-adhesive foam spacers. Weave jute string around letters on border. Using an oval cutting system, cut two oval frames from yellow and red cardstock. Vertically tear red oval cardstock frame in half as shown; layer over yellow cardstock frame with self-adhesive foam spacers. Mount photo behind oval mat. Mount colorful fishing lures on border strips and photo mat; mount fishing pole on red border strip. Print journaling on white cardstock; tear edges and gently curl with fingers.

Kelli Noto

Bathtub

Frame a photo with ceramic tiles

Kelli's unique family portrait, set in a bathtub full of bubbles, is framed with with rows of shiny ceramic tiles as a thematic dimensional embellishment. Mat photos on black cardstock. Double mat large photo, leaving room for border embellishment. Mount tiles at top and bottom of second matting. Print title and journaling on gray cardstock; mat on black cardstock. Mount matted photos and journaling on blue background cardstock.

I hide behind the camera and collect little 4 x 6" slices of life to call my own. I put these little rectangles into scrapbooks so I can show my children how much they are loved. There are very rarely any photos of me, unless I accidentally shoot my own shadow.

Kelli Noto

Swim

Hook a fish border

Tiny fish charms playfully dangle from small metal hooks under a beaded wire frame. Mat photos on light blue cardstock; mount at bottom of page. Mount two photos on one piece of light blue cardstock, leaving room for title and embellishment. Punch title letters; heat emboss with blue embossing powder. Mount title letters between two photos. Cut wire long enough to frame around both photos; string with beads. Mount beaded wire around photos as shown. Secure beaded frame with ½" pieces of wire bent into a U-shape; place wire over beaded wire and push ends through cardstock to back of page. Twist wire together on back of page to secure; press ends and flatten against page. Attach fish charms to metal hooks; mount under beaded frame with glue dots.

Kelli Noto

I love clay! It's economical and versatile. I can control its bulkiness as well as color it with rub-ons, embossing powders, stamp it, leave it plain. It's great for a title, like the "Baby" on this page or for other embellishments.

Katherine Brooks

Baby

Mold embossed clay letters

Embossed and stamped letters formed from clay headline Katherine's story. Double mat a 10⅞" square piece of patterned paper on green and mustard cardstock; attach small brads at corners of patterned paper. Mat photos and mount on patterned paper. Stamp upper left and lower right corners of left page with geometric pattern. Print journaling on cream cardstock; cut to size. Press edges on ink pad and detail with black pen. Mat small photos on green cardstock; mount at bottom of journaling block. Using a craft knife and straight-edge ruler, slice a ½" frame from green cardstock; slice a ⅜" frame from patterned paper. Layer together and wrap with copper wire. Mount over large photo with self-adhesive foam spacers. Mold polymer clay into a large rectangle. Cut title letters from clay. Heat emboss with copper ultra thick embossing enamel; while enamel is still warm press in patterned stamp. Mount on page above journaling block.

Katherine Brooks

Sea Glass Beach

Sculpt wire into freeform designs

Torrey incorporates contemporary wire designs embellished with glass beads. Stamp seashells and dots on background with watermark stamp for a subtle patterned background; mat on teal cardstock. Mat photos on white cardstock; mount on page. Print title and journaling on patterned vellum. Tear strips of blue and green vellum. Cut wire and bend and curl into freeform shape; string beads as you proceed. Mount atop torn vellum strips as shown. Using a craft knife, slice a window for 3-D keeper; fill with collected sea glass and seal on back. Cut a frame to fit around 3-D keeper from green cardstock.

October 2001
Mom and I stopped at this secluded little beach. We named it "Sea glass Beach" because that's what we found scattered on the shore... We found greens (pale, emerald, seafoam, and olive), turquoise, white, amber, cobalt, and I even found a dark purple piece. It was an unseasonably warm, fall afternoon. What a nice way to end our East Coast adventure.

Most often, a page theme and photos dictate the embellishments on a spread. However, there have been times when I knew that I wanted to try a new embellishment technique and shot photos that would work specifically with it. You use a different part of your brain when you work in that direction.

Torrey Miller

Torrey Miller

Scrapbooking allows me to combine all the crafts I love, including needlework and paper arts, resulting in a page I will treasure forever.

Diana Hudson

Home

Collage decorative elements

Diana's collection of decorative elements is displayed on a crafted memo board. Cover matte board with color copied blueprints; wrap around edges and mount to back of board. Cut ribbon strips; mount diagonally, securing ends to back of board. Attach flower nailheads at ribbon intersections. Before matting black background cardstock on gray cardstock, paper press edges in gold ink. Mount memo board to top of black cardstock. Stamp house design on white cardstock with blue ink; cut to size and press edges onto blue ink pad. Mount metal letter at lower left corner before securing under ribbon. Tie clock charm with embroidery thread; dangle from ribbon. Mount laminate chips, fabric swatch and clipped paint color cards on board, securing under ribbon as shown. Mount glass "love" pebble atop small tassels. Print part of title on gray cardstock; cut into tag shape. Cut large title letters from burgundy cardstock; mount on tag. Press edges of tag onto blue ink pad for decorative edging. Attach eyelet over small blue cardstock strip; tie with burgundy ribbon. Mount small photos behind metal frames; tie with burgundy ribbon before mounting to page. Punch photos into square and rectangle shapes; mount on right page.

Diana Hudson

He's Leaving on a Jet Plane

Embellish a torn frame with baubles

Words could not describe how hard it was for Holle to say goodbye to her husband for a year of service overseas. She does her best with a collage of photos, thematic patterned paper pieces and strips of torn cardstock. Cut pieces of patterned paper along design lines; collage with torn pieces of colored cardstock over burgundy and brown cardstock backgrounds. Die cut title letters from brown and blue cardstock; assemble at the top of both pages. Mat photos on blue and tan cardstock; tear one edge before mounting on collaged background. Print journaling; paper tear edges and mount on page with silver star brads. Tear out center of corrugated cardstock; adhere focal photo behind torn window. Embellish with letter pebbles, beads and patterned paper strips. Wrap corners with wire before mounting at center of right page.

Holle Wiktorek

I don't care if others see a page as "busy" as long as I like it. We all view art through different eyes. I believe that what is really important is making sure that you have a strong title and focal picture on every spread.

Holle Wiktorek

live

love

laugh

Alex at Beckwith Park, July 1st, 2001

Children will not remember you for the material things you provided,

but for the feeling that you cherished them.

- Unknown

Paper

The art of paper making dates back to over 5,000 years ago when Egyptians experimented with cutting and layering thin, softened strips of a plant called Cyperous Papyrus. The plant's strips were pounded into a thin sheet and left in the sun to dry, becoming the perfect medium for record keeping, spiritual texts and works of art. Paper-making techniques progressed throughout the years and continents, working its way through Asia and the Muslim world, Europe and then westward to America. Johann Gutenberg, in the late 15th century, is credited with the birth of "modern paper." Paper making became industrialized in the 19th century and as it became more easily accessible, it proved to be a versatile medium for writers, artists, educators and designers.

Modern scrapbookers are now graced with a large variety of papers for both backgrounds and embellishments. The number of colors and textures available, let alone quality, makes paper THE invaluable source for scrapbookers. Linen, mulberry, vellum, textured or handmade, its uses are limited only by the imagination. We can roll it, texture it, tear it, distress it, layer it, weave it, fold it, stitch it, punch it and emboss it! Enjoy what the Masters have done with paper and see what unique designs you can be inspired to create.

Maize Maze
Layer a-mazing paper crafted cornstalks

Torrey's paper crafted corn maze opens up to reveal two pages of photos. Create the cover with a 12 x 12" piece of moss green cardstock. Cut a 10 x 12" piece of green cardstock; trim top into a wavy line. Vertically layer with $1\frac{1}{4}$" strips of light green cardstock mounted at $\frac{3}{4}$" increments; trim tops along wavy edge. Vertically slice entire page $7\frac{1}{2}$" from left edge, creating the doors for page. Reposition pages together until cover is finished. Freehand cut leaves and corn husks from green cardstock. Bend leaves; mount some with self-adhesive foam spacers. Detail corn husks with chalk; mount atop each other with self-adhesive foam spacers. Mount fibers behind tops of husks. Cut title letters from mustard cardstock; mount on $5\frac{3}{4}$ x $2\frac{3}{4}$" moss green cardstock strip. Vertically slice title block down the middle before mounting on both sides of cover with self-adhesive foam spacers. Set cover "doors" aside. Slice $7\frac{1}{2}$" and $4\frac{1}{2}$" strips of green cardstock for insides of page "doors." Starting with the "door" panels, freehand slice maze design from mustard card-

Torrey Miller

stock using a craft knife and straight-edge ruler. Print journaling on vellum; paper tear and mount over maze design on left "door" panel. Mount torn vellum strips over maze design with single matted photo on right "door" panel. Quadruple mat photo; tear top edge of last mat. Vertically mount fibers alongside photos on both panels. Cut date, names and balance of title from mustard cardstock. Mount date alongside photo. Single and double mat photos for center of fold-out page; tear one edge of second matting. Horizontally mount fibers at middle of page under title words on green cardstock strip. Mount names over torn vellum strips. Attach three 1 x 3" strips of light green cardstock to each side of back of center panel; position at top, center and bottom of page to serve as hinges. Mount front and back panels of left and right "doors" together over hinge strips.

Remember
Pave a pebbled pathway

Valerie crafts a detailed pebble pathway. Mat photos on tan cardstock; tear edges and brush with rust chalk before mounting on page. Stamp title on cream cardstock; embellish with torn cardstock, mulberry and handmade paper strips, mesh and freehand cut pebbles detailed with chalk. Wrap title block with fibers. Tear tan cardstock into path; layer over feather cut torn green cardstock to resemble blades of grass. Detail feathered edges with yellow chalk. Freehand cut pebbles from cardstock in shades of brown; shade with rust and brown chalks and mount along paper-torn pathway.

Valerie Barton

I have learned not to be afraid to expand my horizons beyond traditional scrapbooking. I belong to a local rubber stamp club and get so many new and unique ideas to use in my scrapbooks. When we share and learn creatively from each other, we all come out the better for it.

Valerie Barton

No Yucky Stuff

Layer an intricate freehand-cut design

Torrey re-creates the cow from a yogurt container into a clever design element. Slice large brown and blue cardstock strips; tear one edge. Vertically and horizontally layer over mustard cardstock matted with blue cardstock for background. Freehand draw cow head on brown velveteen paper; silhouette cut. Cut darker areas from cardstock and velveteen papers in shades of brown; layer pieces together to shape cow's face. Mount completed cow at left side of left page with self-adhesive foam spacers. Freehand cut spoon from silver cardstock; add shaded details cut from gray cardstock. Print title and journaling on cream cardstock and vellum. Cut title on cream cardstock into conversation bubble; mat and silhouette cut. Mount on page above cow with self-adhesive foam spacers. Cut journaling block to size; mount on page with small brads at corners. Die-cut "m's" from blue, mustard and brown cardstock. Slice a few and layer colors together for a visually interesting border. Single and double mat photos. Silhouette cut large photo; mount at bottom of page amongst die-cut "m's".

Torrey Miller

My entire family supports me in my scrapbooking obsession...my dad, sister and aunt faithfully and eagerly anticipate all my creations. And above all, none of this would be possible without the gifts that God has so graciously given me.

Torrey Miller

Dandelions

Punch and layer dimensional flowers

Torrey illustrates the life of a dandelion
with punched shapes. Mat photos on yel-
low cardstock; mount atop mustard cardstock background. Write poem on yellow cardstock; cut to
size and mount on page. Craft dandelion flowers from sun and flower shapes punched from yellow,
tan and green cardstock and vellum. Freehand cut stems from brown cardstock. Layer among freehand cut cardstock leaves and grass. Punch large sun shapes; layer with punched flower shapes
using self-adhesive foam spacers between layers. Gently bend top layer of punched flowers. Punch
small leaves from green cardstock; layer and mount over small sun punched from vellum and yellow cardstock for flower buds. Craft vellum dandelion fly-aways from punched sun shapes; trim off
segments with small scissors and layer with freehand-cut brown cardstock stems. Randomly mount
dandelion fly-aways on pages.

Torrey Miller

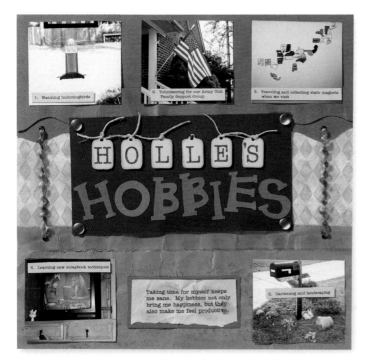

Holle Wiktorek

Holle's Hobbies

Texture and distress cardstock

Holle's hobbies include scrapbooking those hobbies, as seen on
this diverse page. Cut one $4\frac{1}{2}$ x 12" piece of brown paper using
a wavy template on one side; mount at top of patterned background paper. Cut one side of a $1\frac{1}{4}$" strip of brown paper using
wavy template; mount atop large brown paper strip. Distress rust
cardstock by crumpling and flattening; rub with brown and
black chalk. Slice two $3\frac{1}{2}$ x 12" strips of distressed cardstock;
layer at bottom of page. Attach eyelets 1" from edge of each side
and 4" from the top and bottom of page. String fibers through
eyelets; secure at back of page. Crop photos into squares; mount
at top and bottom of page. Print title, journaling and photo captions on tan paper; cut to size. Mount photo captions on photos.
Crumple and flatten journaling block; tear bottom edge and distress with chalk and ink before matting on brown cardstock. Cut
title letters into small tags; punch hole at top; tie with twine and
chalk edges. Mount tags on $4\frac{1}{4}$ x $7\frac{3}{4}$" piece of black cardstock.
Cut large title letters from brown cardstock; mount under title
tags. Attach title block to page with large gold brads at corners.

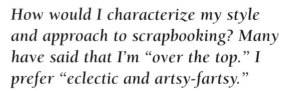

How would I characterize my style and approach to scrapbooking? Many have said that I'm "over the top." I prefer "eclectic and artsy-fartsy."

Torrey Miller

Clara

Dry emboss on vellum

Dry embossed leaves enhance Torrey's heritage photos. Punch twelve 1" squares from blue cardstock and eight 1" squares from teal cardstock; punch decorative corner at one corner of each square. Layer patterned paper with decorative punched corners over blue decorative corners and mat on teal cardstock for background. Using a craft knife and straightedge ruler, slice a 2½ x 5½" window in a 5½ x 9" cream cardstock frame. Slice a 3 x 6" window in a 4¾ x 8½" patterned paper frame and a 5 x 8⅝" blue cardstock frame. Layer patterned paper frame and blue cardstock frame together over decorative punched corners at insides of window; mount atop cream cardstock frame and photo. Print title on vellum and cut to size; mount on blue cardstock trimmed with decorative corner punches and photo slots. Using a graduated template, cut ovals into cream and teal cardstock and patterned paper to frame photo. Slice windows into mat as described above for photo on right page slightly off-center; mount together over blue decorative photo corners. Print journaling on cream vellum trimmed with decorative scissors. Freehand dry emboss leaves to match patterned paper design on cream vellum. Use a stylus and a mouse pad to emboss. Trim around leaves with decorative scissors. Mount leaves on blue cardstock with decorative punched corners; layer atop blue decorative punched corner squares before mounting on pages.

Torrey Miller

Peter Rabbit

Re-create a storytime favorite

Torrey crafts a picture book hero from paper. Triple mat photo on white, cream and beige cardstock. Punch decorative corner into cream cardstock mat before layering over small teal squares. Mount matted photo on teal cardstock matted with beige cardstock with punched decorative corners. Punch two 1½" square from beige cardstock; trim corners with decorative corner punch. Slice in half and embellish cream photo mat. Print title block on cream cardstock; cut to size and punch decorative corners. Mat on beige cardstock before mounting on page. Freehand draw rabbit, jacket and carrots on colored cardstock. Silhouette cut drawn pieces; detail with pen and chalk. Piece together and mat on tan cardstock; silhouette cut around design. Weave basket from ¼" strips of brown and tan cardstock. Freehand cut, bend and mount basket handle. Trim woven rectangle into basket shape and detail with pen and chalk. Layer carrots behind basket. Mount rabbit and basket around title block with self-adhesive foam spacers.

Torrey Miller

The View

Layer patterned papers

Diana layers patterned vellum and paper together for a muted background that brings focus to the photo. Print partial title and journaling on patterned paper. Cut a 6 x 12" piece of patterned vellum; mount on top half of patterned paper for background. Print journaling on 7¾ x 10" olive green cardstock; mount photo and layer on background papers. Slice a ¼" strip of patterned vellum; horizontally mount 1¼" from bottom of page. Adhere letter stickers on photo/journaling block and patterned paper background as shown. Mount plastic window over dried leaf and mesh scrap with copper brads.

Diana Hudson

Wedding Memories

Fold decorative paper frames

Holle's pleated photo frames add a subtle decorative element to wedding photos. Silhouette cut preprinted frames; write journaling with gold and green pens. Print journaling on printed vellum; cut to size and mount on pink paper before mounting atop preprinted frames. Craft folded photo frames from patterned paper by first cutting a 2¼ x 3½" window into a 4¼ x 5½" piece of patterned paper. Miter corners with a straightedge ruler and craft knife, cutting a ½" slice at a 45 degree angle toward the outside of the frame. Fold pleats at ¼" increments in a back and forth fashion after scoring with a bone folder and straightedge ruler.

Holle Wiktorek

Family

Paper tear title and photo mats

Paper-torn photo and journaling mats keep Brandi's page looking soft while adding a textured accent. Slice a 4½" strip of patterned paper; tear one edge and mount vertically over pink paper background as a border. Print title and journaling on ivory cardstock; cut to size and mat on patterned paper with paper-torn edges. Link title letters together with small pieces of wire pushed through page and secured at back. Layer ivory cardstock over patterned paper; tear edges and use as photo mat.

Brandi Ginn

I know that my scrapbooking style has been called "shabby chic." While that's often the case—I like to create pages that include scrunched and rolled paper, stitching, a weathered look and nontraditional elements, I don't think that this page fits the definition. It's not "shabby," just "chic"!

Trudy Sigurdson

Trudy Sigurdson

Tia and Trudy

Weave wavy strips

Trudy constructs a textured background with loosely woven wavy cardstock strips. Freehand cut wavy strips from pink and mauve cardstock. Weave together over white cardstock, starting at the upper left corner. Secure ends; attach eyelets at corners. Double mat photos on pink and mauve cardstock. Mount large photo on left page with photo corners; outline with black fine-tip pen. Print journaling on pink cardstock; cut to size, mat and outline with black fine-tip pen. Cut tags from white cardstock; stamp names, adhere heart stickers and outline with black fine-tip pen. Attach eyelet and tie sheer ribbon. Mount glass pebble atop heart stickers. Attach swirl clip to tag with dragonfly charm. Layer skeleton leaves, mica tiles, dragonfly charms, metal heart and star, and embellished tags over woven background and around photos and journaling blocks.

Trains in a Bubble

Punch a landscaped border

Heidi re-creates the charming atmosphere of a model train yard with punched flowers and leaves layered as a border accent. Slice two $\frac{1}{4}$" strips of burgundy cardstock; vertically mount at edges of forest green cardstock background. Print title and journaling on cream and brown cardstock. Cut title border strip; mat on brown cardstock. Horizontally mount on background. Cut small title words on brown cardstock to size; mount on title strip and embellish with punched flower. Silhouette cut photo element; mount at end of title strip. Double mat photos on cream and brown cardstock, leaving room on first mat for embellishments. Paper tear brown and gray "pebbles" from cardstock; mount on title block and photo mats as shown. Adhere train tracks on photo mats with strong adhesive. Punch flowers, leaves and grass from colored cardstock; layer and mount at top and bottom of page as a border.

Heidi Schueller

Punches are an expensive investment, so when I buy a punch (and I only own 9-10), I select those that I'm sure I'll use over and over. For example, I own a couple of snowflake punches because I live in Wisconsin and I'm certain I'll have plenty of winter pages to create.

Heidi Schueller

Tootsie

Punch a colorful flower lei

Torrey adds an elegant punched lei around a vintage photo as a decorative element. Double mat burgundy cardstock with green and yellow cardstocks; punch corners of burgundy and green cardstocks with decorative corner punch. Quadruple mat photo with white, purple and green cardstocks. Craft photo corners with 1¾" squares cut from purple cardstock. Punch opposite corners with decorative corner punch; layer punched design over lavender cardstock. Diagonally slice square in half; mount decorative corner over photo and fold edges behind matting and secure. Mat photo two more times on green cardstock with punched decorative corners and yellow cardstock. Print title and journaling on lavender cardstock; cut to size and trim edges with decorative scissors. Double mat title block and mount atop multi-matted photo. Punch flowers from colored cardstocks; layer and mount to form a flower lei.

Torrey Miller

A Sweet Proposal

Feature torn flowers

Valerie's paper-torn flowers add elegance to her page. Tear a 4" strip of patterned paper; horizontally mount at top of light green cardstock. Freehand cut tag from green and blue cardstock, sizing one tag just larger than the other; stamp title letter with burgundy ink. Print second title word and journaling on light yellow vellum. Circle cut title word; mount atop metal-rimmed tag and embellish with paper torn flower petals. Attach eyelets to tags and tie fibers. Die cut last title word from burgundy and dark green cardstock. Tear a 3½"-wide strip of patterned paper; vertically mount at right side of right page. Tear a 1" strip of dark blue and burgundy cardstock; vertically mount on either side of patterned paper strip. Mat photo and mount over torn border strips. Tear edges of vellum with printed journaling; tear small hole in vellum to highlight photo element before layering over torn border. Attach eyelets at top and bottom of vellum; string with fibers and tie. Double mat large photo on burgundy and dark green cardstock with torn edges. Double mat photos for right page; tear second mat of two photos. Freehand tear flower petals from colored cardstock and assemble to look like flowers in patterned paper. Layer on page with freehand sliced stems and torn leaves.

Valerie Barton

She's Got Personality

Embellish journaling tags

Diana nestles embellished journaling tags inside of decorative envelopes. Mat blue paper on green paper for background. Layer a 7 x 11½" piece of patterned paper with one torn edge over background. Mat photos on teal, purple and green papers. Print part of title and journaling on white cardstock. Cut title words into small tag shapes. Attach eyelets and tie with embroidery thread. Die cut title letters from white cardstock; mount at top of page and detail with blue chalk. Cut journaling blocks into large tag shapes; add pen details around the edges. Attach eyelets at tops of tags; tie embroidery threads with beads and number charm. Embellish tags with flower eyelets before nestling in embellished vellum envelopes. Fold vellum into envelopes using template. Stitch to page with white embroidery thread. Embellish envelopes with flower stickers, ricrack and torn patterned paper strips.

Diana Graham

It's easy for me to scrapbook about my kids, but I have difficulty scrapbooking about myself. I guess I'm a little intimidated by the prospect. I know it will be difficult and take time, so I find myself setting the task aside until I feel that I can do it "right."

Diana Graham

Holle Wiktorek

Springtime Smiles

Layer dimensional flowers

Holle picks pre-made dimensional flowers and layers them into pretty springtime bouquets on her photo mats. Mat two photos on purple cardstock; layer third photo under preprinted cardstock frame. Mount on patterned paper background. Print journaling; cut to size and mat on purple cardstock. Wrap bottom of journaling block with fibers before mounting on page. Die cut title letters from purple cardstock; mount at top of page and on photo frame. Layer pre-made embellished flowers at corners of photo mats.

Sugar & Spice

Add a soft touch with torn mulberry

Gently torn mulberry paper contrasts with sharp photo corners, reflecting the two sides of Heidi's little girl. Mat two 10½" squares of navy cardstock on lavender cardstock. Layer over patterned background paper, leaving inside edge flush with patterned paper. Cut two 1" squares from yellow patterned paper; slice diagonally and mount as corners of matted navy cardstock. Double mat photos on yellow patterned paper and pastel colored mulberry paper, tearing edges by using a thin paintbrush and small amount of water to paint a line along mulberry paper. Gently pull apart to create feathered edges. Cut or punch 1" squares from patterned paper and 1¼" squares from lavender cardstock; slice all diagonally and layer as photo corners. Print title and flower clip art from computer; silhouette cut. Layer a few flowers with vellum; silhouette cut around shape and mount at photo corners and along bottom of navy cardstock. Mount title letters at top of navy cardstock. Layer preprinted butterfly die cuts with vellum; silhouette cut and mount on page.

I come from a long line of artists. My grandma wanted to be a fashion designer and my mother earned her degree in Fine Arts. I earned my degree in Fine Arts as well and continue to draw and paint whenever I get the chance. But since I have little girls, I can't help adding to their beauty by creating memorable scrapbook pages around their photos!

Heidi Schueller

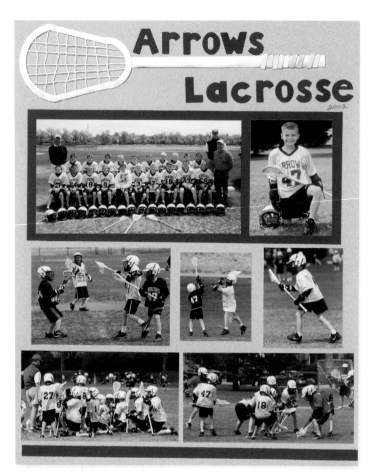

Arrows Lacrosse
Craft realistic sports equipment

Kelli gives realistic detail to a paper crafted lacrosse hook with string and dimensional chalking. Mat two photos on one black mat. Slice a $\frac{1}{4}$" strip of black cardstock; horizontally mount at bottom of page. Crop remaining photos and mount on gray cardstock background. Punch title letters from black cardstock; mount at top of page. Craft lacrosse hook from paper and string. Freehand cut curved and straight pieces for net; mount rows of string behind assembled hook pieces as shown. Slice $\frac{1}{8}$" and $\frac{3}{8}$" strips of white cardstock; wrap $\frac{1}{8}$" strip around end of $\frac{3}{8}$" strip as shown. Shade with gray chalk. Crop photos for right hand page. Lay sections of mesh on gray cardstock background page. Mount photos and journaling block on mesh, allowing portions of the mesh to show.

Kelli Noto

I've found that if I want action shots of a sports event I get better pictures when I shoot the warm-ups than the game itself. When photographing the warm-ups I can get closer and it is easier to anticipate the action and know where the ball is going to be. That makes it easier to follow it with my camera.

Kelli Noto

Kelli Noto

Hoops

Give basketball stickers a little bounce

Punched squares, layered with foam spacers add dimension to basketball stickers. Slice a 2¾"-wide strip of black cardstock; vertically mount at left side of brown cardstock background. Adhere basketball stickers on black border; punch 1½" squares into sticker border. Mat punched squares on 1¾" white cardstock squares with self-adhesive foam spacer. Mount dimensionally matted squares back over punched area, making sure to line up basketball lines. Punch 1¼" and 1½" squares from brown and white cardstock for title. Mount brown cardstock squares atop white cardstock squares with self-adhesive foam spacers. Randomly slice letter stickers; mount letter sticker segments on dimensional squares and brown background. Cut journaling blocks and mat; journal with black pen.

Tough Yet Tender

Weave a simple border design

Valerie adds visual interest to title borders with a woven design. Slice a 2½" x 11¼" strip from blue cardstock and a 2½ x 9¼" strip from burgundy cardstock; set burgundy strip aside. Using a craft knife and straightedge ruler, slice into blue cardstock to prepare for weaving. Starting ¼" from side edge and 3" from one end of blue cardstock, slice nine 3" strips at ¼" increments, cutting all the way to end of cardstock strip. Slice seven ¼ x 3½" strips of burgundy cardstock. Weave burgundy strips into blue cardstock in under/over fashion, leaving ¼" between each woven strip. Secure ends with adhesive and trim off excess. Vertically mount completed woven border strip at left side of page as border on black cardstock background; horizontally mount burgundy border strip at bottom of page. Cut title letters from crumpled and flattened brown cardstock; detail with gold metallic rub-ons and black chalk around the edges. Attach eyelets to a few letters; mount title word on blue cardstock strip. Die cut shadowed title word from brown and white mulberry paper; layer and mount on burgundy cardstock. Write remaining title word on small tag; shade tag with chalk and tie with jute string. Mount with small clothespin where two border strips meet. Print journaling on vellum; paper tear edges. Layer with cropped photos on page. Slice ⅜" burgundy strip and ¼" blue cardstock strip; frame one photo with strips as shown. Paper tear strip of brown distressed cardstock. Insert one corner of mounted photo into sliced paper strip. Freehand craft dandelion from white mulberry paper. Cut small squares of mulberry paper; dampen one edge with water and pull out center to fray edges. Mount pieces together in circle as shown over thin strip of green cardstock.

Valerie Barton

Lucky Fish
Hang vellum paper lanterns

Illuminated paper lanterns hang at the top of Torrey's page documenting a visit to Boston's Chinatown. Double mat gray cardstock with mustard and burgundy cardstock. Double and triple mat photos; mount on page. Print journaling on vellum; cut to size and mount on page with small brads at corners. Freehand craft lanterns from crimped vellum cut into shapes; cut lantern handles and bottoms from brown cardstock. Mount with crimped vellum shapes over freehand cut and layered flames with self-adhesive foam spacers. "Hang" lanterns on fiber; horizontally mount fiber across top of page. Freehand cut triangles to shape into title letters; mount on lanterns and sliced vellum strip. Freehand cut and color large fish from tan cardstock. Detail with pen and chalks; mount on page with self-adhesive foam spacers.

Torrey Miller

Reflections of Albuquerque
Assemble a mosaic from punched shapes

Torrey re-creates a detailed mosaic from punched shapes. Mat blue cardstock on brown cardstock. Cut a 5¼" strip of beige cardstock; horizontally mount at center of page. Slice ¼", 1" and 2¼" strips of tan vellum; mount at top of page and above and below beige cardstock. Punch squares, rectangles and triangles from colored cardstock. Assemble on vellum strips in a mosaic design similar to that in photo. Triple mat photos on white, rust and brown cardstock; mount on page. Print journaling on vellum; cut to size and mount on blue cardstock background. Freehand draw and cut design from rust and beige cardstock; layer with punched circles at bottom of journaling block.

Torrey Miller

Valentine's Day Weekend

Roll torn edges of photo mats

Holle layers matted photos with torn and rolled edges over strips of stamped and torn cardstock for a rustic look. Stamp state name on yellow and brown cardstock and vellum with brown inks. Tear stamped cardstock and vellum into large pieces; collage over blue background cardstock. Single and double mat photos on brown and green cardstock; tear edges of first mat. Gently curl torn edges. Frame one photo with frayed material scrap mounted on page. Mount stitched buttons around fiber framed photo and at top of page with cork strip. Paper tear hearts from red cardstock; brush edges with brown and black chalk. Die cut title letters from dark green cardstock; layer over paper-torn hearts. Cut last title word from corrugated cardstock using template; mount along bottom of page. Print journaling on rust cardstock; tear edges and mount on page.

When I started teaching I realized I changed my bulletin boards more than any teacher in the school. When scrapbooking was introduced professionally in Tennessee I realized my scrapbook pages were "mini bulletin boards."

Holle Wiktorek

Holle Wiktorek

It's the Little Moments

Texture a multilayered photo frame

Katherine highlights a favorite photo behind multilayered, textured and inked photo mats. Slice two $\frac{1}{4}$" strips of olive green and brown cardstock and one $\frac{1}{2}$" strip of rust cardstock. Horizontally mount at bottom of pages. Mount brads on rust strip at 3" increments. Crumple and flatten an $8\frac{1}{2}$ x 11" piece of green cardstock; dab brown and bronze ink over cardstock with a crumpled paper towel. Using a craft knife and straightedge ruler, cut a 6 x $8\frac{1}{2}$" window in textured and inked cardstock. Cut smaller windows in rust, olive green and tan cardstocks; tear inside edges of olive green frame. Mount green textured frame over smaller frames with foam tape. Curl inside torn edges of olive green matting toward outside of page. Print title on vellum; cut into strip and mount at bottom of multi-matted photo with brass clips. Double mat photos for right page. Print journaling on tan cardstock; cut to size. Punch holes in three journaling strips; tie with fibers and mount all on page.

it's the little moments that make my heart melt

Katherine Brooks

I kept all of my scrapbooking supplies in a small plastic bin when I first started. Now, several years later, I have my own room along with several cabinets in the kitchen!

Katherine Brooks

Christmas in the Desert

Ink edges of cardstock

Katherine adds a bit of color to page elements by carefully pressing their edges on a colored ink pad. Mat moss green cardstock with brown cardstock. Mat three photos on olive green cardstock; cut to size, leaving room for title blocks. Press edges of matting on ink pad to shade. Mat four photos on brown cardstock; mount two at bottom of left page and two at top of right page. Freehand cut tag from tan cardstock; press edges on ink pad to shade. Punch hole in punched tan cardstock circle at top of tag; tie with fibers. Stamp date on small white tag, crumple, flatten and rub with chalk. Tie string to top of small tag and attach to present. Crumple, flatten and shade die-cut cactus; mount with pre-made present atop large tag. Print title and journaling on light and olive green cardstock. Cut title blocks to size; press edges on ink pad. Mount at bottom of large photo mat with small brads. Cut journaling into a 2¾" strip; horizontally mount at right side of right page. Using a craft knife and ruler, slice a 5½ x 3⅜" window in a 6¼ x 4¼" piece of olive green cardstock. Press outside edges of frame on ink pad. Cut a 5¼ x 3⅜" window in a 6 x 4" piece of light green cardstock. Mount olive green frame over light green frame; tie with fibers on right side. Mount frame over photo on page with self-adhesive foam spacers.

Katherine Brooks

Friday's Child

Embellish torn cardstock strips

Torrey assembles a simple monochromatic page to accentuate striking photos. Stamp chicken wire design on light green cardstock with watermark stamp ink for a subtle background pattern; mat with dark green cardstock. Print journaling on light green cardstock strip; horizontally tear and mount as a 2½"-wide border strip near bottom of page. Tear another 2½" strip of light green cardstock; vertically mount over stamped cardstock background as shown. Print title on green vellum; tear into strip and layer on page wrapping one end around stamped background. Mount sheer ribbon atop torn cardstock strips; wrap ends around to back of page and secure. Punch hearts from light and dark green cardstock; mount on torn border strips with self-adhesive foam spacers for dimension. Mat photos and layer on page.

Torrey Miller

Valerie Barton

Our View of Canoeing the Okatoma

Craft a textured river

Valerie creates a textured river bank and hidden journaling blocks on a page documenting a memorable trip on the Okatoma River. Punch 1½" squares from colored cardstock; assemble at top of page in two rows as a border. Mount journaling blocks on cardstock strips. Attach two or four punched squares from border to top of each strip. Slice opening in cardstock background; slide journaling strips through openings. Mount remaining punched squares to background. Stamp title words on squares with brown ink as shown; mount 1" square punched photo vignettes on remaining squares. Mat two photos on blue cardstock over torn light green cardstock strip; tear top and bottom edge of matting. Using a bone folder and straightedge ruler, horizontally score cardstock just under photo and fold up over photo. Machine stitch across photo. Mat remaining photos on colored cardstock; tear bottom edge of one mat. Mount on page over torn blue cardstock strips. Piece together a mosaic river from small paper-torn cardstock scraps layered together. Craft textured river banks with liquid adhesive mixed with pigment powder; mix together on wax paper and sprinkle with sawdust. Let dry overnight; peel off in segments and assemble on either side of mosaic river.

Grant's Farm

Embellish tags with dimensional elements

Brandi stamps and embellishes a series of tags with buttons, wire, paper yarn and a sunny quilled design. Mat two sets of three photos on one strip of brown cardstock; mount at bottom of pages over tan cardstock background. Mat two photos on green and brown cardstocks. Print title and journaling on cream cardstock; cut to size and press edges on ink pad. Stamp designs on precut tags and ink around edges before embellishing. On first tag, mount buttons embellished with curled wire over green torn-paper strips; attach eyelet. For second tag, quill sun from yellow cardstock strip; mount at center of punched flames. Attach eyelet over punched green cardstock circle. Mount buttons over distressed cardstock strip on third tag; attach eyelet over punched brown cardstock square. Glue stitched button over paper yarn looped into flower shape; layer over torn green cardstock on fourth tag. Attach eyelet.

I'm having to buy albums much more often than I used to because the popular bulky embellishments fill them so quickly. Tags are a great way to embellish without bulk, and that saves me money!

Brandi Ginn

We love Grant's Farm! It's so much fun to watch Alexa experience the goats! We learned that when you go in the spring they are so tiny--perfect size for a two year old. The goats barely came up to her waist and they haven't learned to jump on their hind legs and attack anyone with food! Alexa even shared her string cheese with the older goats. Brinley was comfortably asleep in her sling and missed out on everything. Although at 2 months I'm not sure she cared.   April 2001

Brandi Ginn

Metallics

Man first used metals such as gold, copper, lead and silver to create practical items such as weapons and eating utensils. As early as 6,000 B.C., Ancient Egyptians used lead in liquid form as eye paint because of its shiny metallic appearance. The use of metals expanded throughout the Medieval and Renaissance periods in which it was utilized to create armor, to the Gothic period when it was used for architecture, and on to the Art Nouveau arts and crafts movement. Each metal holds its own fascination for man. Gold, symbolic over the ages as a measure of wealth, is malleable and glows with luster. Copper, with its rich tones, is a good conductor of heat and electricity. Lead, the easiest metal to bend and shape while maintaining its strength, is ideal for nuts and bolts. Silver, a softer metal, is perfect for fashioning decorative ornaments, chains and jewelry.

Scrapbookers have recently recognized the many qualities metal can bring to their pages. It reflects and adds color and texture as eyelets, beads, embossing powders, clips, sequins, glitter, pins or studs and brads. Metals can be used for fastening and securing items on a page or simply as an embellishment. You can coil it, form it, emboss it, bend it, shape it, bead it...even wrap it! We're sure that you'll be able to find plenty of metallic inspiration in the following pages to get you thinking about how you can add its shining elements to your layouts.

Torrey Miller

Sand Between Her Toes

Wrap metal hearts with beaded wire

Torrey adds a rustic decorative element with beaded wire wrapped around "rusty" metal hearts. Crumple and flatten brown cardstock for texture; rub with coarse sandpaper for a wind-swept look similar to the sand dunes in the photo. Mat enlarged photo on patterned cardstock, leaving room for embellishments; tear edges and gently curl toward photo with fingers. Vertically slice matted photo to be mounted on both pages. Print journaling on vellum, leaving room for highlighted words. Stamp words on colored cardstock with brown ink; cut or paper tear to size. Mount atop printed vellum, at the side of and on photo mat with self-adhesive foam spacers. Mount vellum on left page; mount matted photo with self-adhesive foam spacers on both pages as shown. Wrap metal hearts with beaded wire as shown; mount over torn teal cardstock strip at right side of photo mat.

A Cherished Love

Add a golden touch with embossing powder

Katherine adds a golden touch to unique page embellishments by embossing with gold embossing powder. Tear a 4½" strip of patterned paper; layer over a larger strip of torn khaki paper. Vertically mount on tan cardstock matted with black cardstock; gently roll torn edges with fingers. Mat photo on black cardstock; layer over layered torn strips. Attach eyelets on either side of photo as shown. Heat emboss metal-rimmed vellum tag with gold embossing powder; stamp letters while embossing powder is still warm. Punch holes in sides of embossed tag; string gingham ribbon through tag and eyelets and tie. Ink edges of premade tags; stamp with title words. Heat emboss metal clock with gold embossing powder; mount on one tag. Tie tags with gingham ribbon; mount at top of page with self-adhesive foam spacers. Print journaling on cream cardstock; cut to size and press edges on ink pad to shade. Punch flowers from white cardstock; attach brads in center and press edges of flower petals on ink pad to shade. Mount flowers atop curled wire as shown.

Katherine Brooks

Explore, Discover

Emboss metal letters

Katherine heats a few layers of ultra thick copper embossing powder to add dimension and shine to metal title letters. Cut moss green cardstock in half; mount over dark green cardstock for background. Horizontally attach mesh strip at center of page; wrap around ends of page and secure on back. Double mat large photo on left page; use textured cardstock for second mat. Press edges on ink pad to shade. Turn down upper left corner and secure with silver metal star stud. Single and double mat photos on brown, green and textured cardstock. Attach brads between two photos matted on one piece of brown cardstock. Mount double matted photos on page with foam tape for a bit of dimension. Crop remaining small photos into squares and rectangles; lightly distress the edges with sandpaper and mount along the top of both pages as shown. Heat emboss metal letters by pressing letter on an embossing pad; sprinkle with copper embossing powder. Repeat until desired thickness is achieved. Heat from underneath until bubbly; mount on page when cooled. Press ink pad on white cardstock; print journaling on inked white cardstock. Cut to size and tear edges; gently curl torn edges with fingers. Stamp date at bottom of right page with black ink.

I love trying new techniques and capturing not just major events, but those fun silly moments I never want to forget.

Katherine Brooks

Katherine Brooks

Two Little Souls...

String beads on coiled wire

Brandi adds sparkle and shine that is second only to the smiles on her daughters' faces with strands of beaded coiled wire. Mount photos together across bottom of one page and across the top of the other. String large and small beads on coiled wire; mount along photos. Secure large beads to page with glue dots. Mount small photos behind metal frames; layer over beaded coiled wire strands. Single and double mat remaining photos on blue cardstock and mesh fabric; mount at corners. Print journaling; cut to size and mount below one matted photo on fabric.

Brandi Ginn

I am the granddaughter of a photographer and grew up in front of the camera. Winning a camera (in a photo contest in 1992) sparked my interest in taking pictures. Scrapbooking, for me, was the natural extension of the creative process.

Brandi Ginn

I consider myself visually, rather than verbally creative, so I often can't come up with words that express what I feel. That's why I use poems and quotes on my pages. I often know what kind of thing I want to say, but it may take me hours to find the right verse. I think that the poem I pick is equally as important as the photos and can make or break a page.

Trudy Sigurdson

Trudy Sigurdson

Cherished

Add dimension to metallic stickers

Trudy gives extra dimension to pewter stickers by mounting them on wooden blocks before adding them as an embellishment to her page. Double mat photos with light and dark blue textured cardstock; mount over light blue matted cardstock background with photo corners. Print title and date on light blue textured cardstock and poem on vellum. Cut title and journaling strip to size, crumple and flatten. Mat on dark blue cardstock strip; attach small silver brad on one side. Mount both on page over skeleton leaf. Cut printed vellum to size. String pewter beads on fibers; mount at top and bottom of printed vellum strip. Adhere pewter stickers atop small wooden blocks; mount at one side of title and journaling blocks and over skeleton leaves on vellum.

Diana Graham

By the Shore
Tell a story with metal word eyelets

Diana assembles a sentiment about a father-son relationship with metal word eyelets attached to a large handcrafted and embellished tag. Mat patterned paper with green cardstock. Single and double mat photos with blue cardstock and green patterned paper. Mount metal photo corners on double matted photo. Layer single matted photo with mesh scrap. Print part of title and journaling on blue and white cardstock. Cut title word block to size and mount behind metal frame next to metal title letters. Cut date journaling to size; mount under green glass pebble at bottom right corner of page next to metal number eyelets. Freehand cut tag from green patterned paper; attach eyelet at top over circle punched screen. Tie unwrapped paper yarn to tag. Tear small holes in tag; mount mesh behind torn holes. Mount metal frame on tag over cropped photo. Assemble metal word eyelets with printed and cut words into sentiment on tag. Shade pail and shovel die cuts with chalks for dimension. Cover torn paper strips with decorative sand using two sided tape; mount above and below sand pail with sand dollars and sea stars.

Grandma
Dangle metal frame charms

Miniature gold frames dangle from a decorative metal plaque as an elegant page embellishment. Mat enlarged photo on patterned paper; layer with frame sliced from green cardstock over cream cardstock background. Print journaling on vellum and title on green cardstock. Silhouette cut title and mount at top of page. Cut journaling block to size; mount alongside photo as shown. Write journaling on light green cardstock; cut to size to fit behind small metal frame charms. Tie frame charms with thin green ribbon; secure ends under decorative metal plaque mounted on page.

My grandmother is full of spirit. She laughs easily, likes telling dirty jokes, and can bake up a storm. . She used to win radio contests on a weekly basis. When my father and his brother were young, they'd run from her when they were in trouble. She chased them down, hurdling over fences with her red hair and skirt flying behind her. She always caught them. Grandma has a very full life. She is so busy with her various activities that it is hard to find a time to take her to lunch. She survived the Great Depression, World War II, raising two rambunctious boys and a spirited daughter, breast cancer, and losing her husband of sixty years. She is a remarkable woman and I am blessed to have her as my grandmother.

Kelli Noto

It's Not Fair!

Dangle wire stars from eyelets

Valerie bends wire into dangling stars that hang from a cut and folded window secured with silver eyelets. Using a decorative ruler, draw a 4½ x 5½" zigzag frame on green cardstock. Slice along penciled lines with a craft knife and straightedge ruler. Bend pointed ends back and secure with eyelets. Paper tear a small window in upper right corner of green cardstock before mounting on gray cardstock background. Adhere pewter sticker at center of torn window on gray cardstock. Mat photo on green cardstock; mount at center of decorative window on gray cardstock. Bend wire into star shapes using a jewelry jig; dangle from eyelets with freehand crafted wire hook. Print journaling on green cardstock; cut to size and mat on gray cardstock before mounting on page.

Valerie Barton

Diana Graham

Fuzzy Caterpillar

Layer metal screen on vellum tags

Metal screen scraps add texture and shine to Diana's layered title tags. Single and double mat photos on green cardstock and vellum; mount metal photo corners on one single matted photo. Scrape edges on first mat of double matted photo with scissors blade. Mount photos on patterned paper background; layer one over metal screen mounted with small silver brads. Punch a 1" square into a 1¼" punched square of green cardstock; layer on metal-rimmed vellum tag over metal screen scrap. Attach metal letter on layered tag with silver brad. Print title words and journaling on green vellum. Paper tear around edges and mount title words next to layered tags at top of page. Tear around edges of journaling block; layer over metal screen secured to page with silver brads. Attach a safety pin embellished with a button and beads at top of journaling block.

Topsy Turvy

Incorporate household items into layout

Unusual household items are incorporated into Kelli's layout, providing both subtle and bold metal accents. A stainless steel outlet cover frames title letters while a scrap of window screen becomes a subtle second mat for an enlarged photo. Slice a 1" strip of black cardstock; attach metal letter nailheads as title before horizontally mounting across top page of on gray speckled cardstock. Mat small photo on black cardstock; mount at right side of title border strip. Double mat enlarged photo on black cardstock and window screen frayed around the edges. Print journaling; cut to size and mat on black cardstock. Place stainless steel outlet cover on page; mark holes with pencil on cardstock for placement of eyelets and holes to punch. Set outlet cover aside; punch small holes on markings using a hole punch and attach eyelets. Mount letter nailheads on black cardstock to show through window of outlet cover. Secure outlet cover on page over nailhead letters with wire tied through eyelets and holes.

Kelli Noto

Torrey Miller

The Blues Diner

Create faux "hammered tin" photo corners

Torrey creates the look of antique "hammered tin" accents by stamping designs into silver metallic embossing enamel. Double and triple mat photo on white, blue and silver cardstocks; mount photos on blue matted cardstock background. Print title and journaling on silver cardstock and vellum. Cut title block to size; mat with blue cardstock. Cut journaling block to size; mount on page with eyelets at corners. Stamp and heat emboss toasters on colored cardstock; silhouette cut and mount along bottom of page. Create faux "hammered tin" accents by pressing embossing pad onto cardstock and sprinkle with silver metallic ultra thick embossing enamel. Heat cardstock from underside with embossing gun until powder liquifies. Add a second and third layer of enamel. While enamel is still warm, press in stamped design. Cut design into squares when cool; diagonally slice into triangles. Mount at corners of triple matted photo and title block.

In the Pits

Stamp design into embossed title letters

Katherine stamps a design into warm metallic embossing enamel giving the look of tire tracks imprinted in silhouette cut title letters. Print title font, silhouette cut. Press letters onto embossing pad; heat emboss with silver and clear embossing powders. While still warm, press in stamp design. Mount on blue cardstock background. Slice two ¼" strips of navy cardstock; vertically mount at outside edges of background. Single mat photos on teal and navy cardstock; mount all on page. Attach screw eyelets at corners of largest photo as shown. Freehand cut small rectangular strips from colored cardstock. Mount along bottom of page with square punched photos matted on white cardstock as a border design. Print journaling blocks on white cardstock. Cut large journal block to size; tear bottom edge. Add pen and chalk details around edges. Craft pocket for memorabilia with navy cardstock mounted on page with foam tape adhered around the edges. Punch square "windows" in navy cardstock; mount square punched matted photo behind one window before adhering pocket to page. Mount journaling block atop navy cardstock; slip memorabilia behind dimensional pocket. Cut small journal block to size; mount on screen scrap with small silver brads. Cut tag from light blue cardstock using template; crumple, flatten and brush with tan chalk for a distressed look. Slice window in center of tag; mount screen with journaling behind window. Attach eyelet; tie with fibers. Add the shine of hardware with washers tied to tag fibers.

Katherine Brooks

I have been scrapbooking more layouts and albums having to do with myself. I want my children to know that I'm not just "Mom" and that I have fears, dreams and goals in my life.

Katherine Brooks

Trudy Sigurdson

Riding the Range

Incorporate chicken wire into background design

Trudy creates a visually arresting background with torn cardboard layered over chicken wire. Tear windows from large cardboard; layer atop chicken wire mounted on tan cardstock. Mat photos on brown cardstock. Print title, journaling and photo captions on tan cardstock. Cut title blocks to size and chalk edges; mount with self-adhesive foam spacers over chicken wire in largest window. Cut journaling and photo captions to size; mount under and around photos. Wrap rusty metal hearts with hemp string; mount in torn windows over chicken wire.

Diana Graham

Giddy-Up

Wrap a frame with charms and beads

Charming silver accents wrap around a weathered photo frame and dangle from a faux suede tag. Scrape edges of brown cardstock background with scissors blade for a distressed look. Vertically mount photo border on brown cardstock background. Attach silver brads at corners of background. Scrape pre-made frame die cut with sandpaper; attach silver brad at left side. Tie hemp string embellished with silver beads, western charms and metal letter charm to brad and wrap around left side of photo frame. Mount embellished frame over photo layered on blue jean patterned paper. Double mat photo on beige and brown cardstocks; distress edges. Mount over photo border. Print journaling on ivory cardstock; cut into tag shape. Antique tag with shades of brown ink blotted with a cotton ball; scrape edges. Attach decorative eyelet; tie fibers and hemp string embellished with silver beads. Mount tag below double-matted photo. Tear strip of tan cardstock for title block. Sand paper, sticker and die cut letters. Mount with barbed wire die cut on title strip; adhere dimensional bandanna and rope stickers.

Fascinated

Add simple silver accents for an elegant touch

A solitary silver star serves as a hanger for a velvet matted photo frame. Slice large window in red velveteen paper to frame enlarged photo. Wrap crushed velvet around pre-made matte board; mount over framed photo. Cut ribbon strip; secure ends behind framed photo. Mount large silver star over ribbon to look like frame is hanging on page. Mount pewter letters under framed photo. Write date on red velvet paper; cut to size and mount behind metal frame secured with silver brads. Pen journaling at bottom of page.

Kelli Noto

Katherine Brooks

I Must

Dangle journaling tags from beaded clips

Katherine's list of things she "must do" are crafted into tags dangling from beaded swirl clips. Stain velvet paper with ink; cut velvet and wrap around a die cut cardstock frame. Mount over photo; embellish with micro beads. Stamp copper strip in ink, dry emboss with letters and heat to discolor. Punch hole in copper strip with eyelet setter and attach to frame with copper brads. Tear a 3½" strip of patterned paper and a 4" strip of brown cardstock; paper tear one edge and vertically mount at left side of cardstock background. Gently roll torn edges of brown cardstock with fingers. Cut small copper strips; fold in half; punch hole with eyelet setter and mount on torn strips with small brads. Attach beaded swirl clips to copper loops. Print journaling on cream cardstock; cut into strips. Press edges of journaling strips onto ink pad to shade and punch small hole at one end. Attach jewelry jump rings through holes and dangle on swirl clips. Print title on brown cardstock; silhouette cut and mount at top of page.

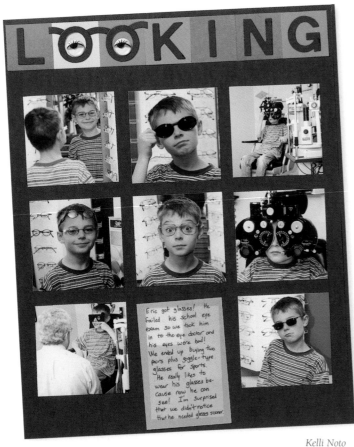

Kelli Noto

I don't carry my camera everywhere, although some people certainly think I do. I limit myself because I found that I was feeling like a spectator in my children's lives instead of a participant. It tends to isolate me from others because I'm only seeing a limited perspective—like when my son was knocked unconscious during a lacrosse game. I didn't see it happen because I was looking through my camera and he was outside my view.

Kelli Noto

Looking Spectacular

Embellish a good lookin' page with playful vellum journaling tags

Kelli creates a dramatic layout with vibrant colors set against a solid black background. Crop photos. Mount eight photos on the left-hand page directly onto black cardstock background. Attach silver brads to the remaining six photos; mount photos on right-hand page. Cut small vellum journaling tags: journal on tags. Set a silver eyelet in each tag. Wrap wire through eyelets and around set brads. Use a template to create the colored title letters. Mount letters on the first page on colorful cardstock blocks. Connect the "O's" in the word "LOOK" with freehand cut paper strips to form glasses. Attach googly eyes inside "O's." Journal on vellum block and attach to page over cardstock colorblock.

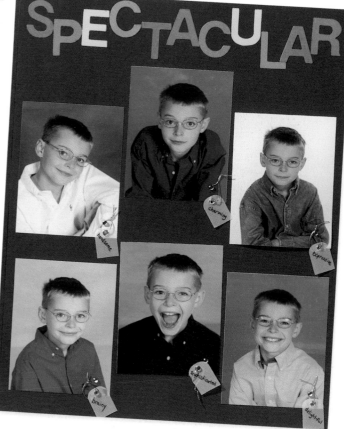

What You Do At 2

Dress up an occasion with a touch of elegant silver

Brandi adds a touch of class to her page with silver frames, adornments and photo corners. Mat one photo on rectangular sand-colored cardstock block. Mat two photos on torn sand strip, gently ripping and curling on edge; mount. Layer vellum over stamped sand paper and cut through both sheets to create title tag. Adhere pieces together. Wrap small rectangular piece of cardstock around one end of tag. Set eyelet through cardstock and tag; tie with fibers. Write title. Mount to background paper. Create journaling tag on the right-hand page in similar manner. Mat remaining photos on stamped paper; mount on background page. Embellish with silver photo corners, paper clip and adornment. Journal sentiment on separate small piece of vellum. Cut to size and mount behind silver frame.

Brandi Ginn

I've been scrapbooking on and off since I was about 10 or 12, and it looked really cheesy. I started to have more fun with it when I got married, almost 7 years ago. I think my overall style is pretty traditional but I love trying new things so my albums, as a whole, can be really eclectic.

Brandi Ginn

Father's Build Dreams

Mount metal with metal

Katherine layers screen under matted photos for a masculine touch to a sentimental page. Stamp dark green cardstock with ink pad for a subtle pattern. Slice two ½" strips and two ¼" strips of inked cardstock and two ¼" strips of light green cardstock. Horizontally mount across top and bottom of rust cardstock background. Mat photos on light green cardstock; layer two matted photos on inked cardstock and large screen scrap. Tear bottom edge of screen; mount on page with flat eyelets. Print journaling on brown cardstock; cut to size and press edges on ink pad to shade. Mat on inked green cardstock. Attach screen scrap at bottom of journaling block with flat eyelets. Mount matted photo with self-adhesive foam spacers at bottom right corner of page. Punch squares into faux leather paper; mount at right side of journaling block. Stamp title letters at bottom of page with brown ink. Heat emboss first title word with silver embossing powder.

Katherine Brooks

Lately, with working and traveling, I find that I can't keep up with my normal 12 x 12" layouts and have started to create smaller albums for each trip.

Katherine Brooks

Haley

Shape wire into freeform flowers

Free-formed flowers shaped into wire embellishments are intertwined with embossed die-cut title letters. Divide burgundy cardstock background into quadrants; cut colored cardstock to fit sections. Double mat photo; trim second mat with decorative scissors and mount on colorblocked background. Die cut letters from burgundy cardstock; outline with embossing pen and heat emboss edges with copper embossing powders. Freehand form wire flowers from thin gauge wire; wrap wire around mounted and embossed title letters. Shape wire into numbers for date. Secure flowers and date to page with small pieces of wire bent into a "U"-shape; pierce holes through cardstock background and insert "U"-pins over wire embellishments. Twist "U"-pin wires together on back of page and flatten to secure wire.

Torrey Miller

Torrey Miller

Timeless

Embellish a paper crafted watch

Torrey paper crafts an antique pocket watch showcasing photos using an interactive spinning template. Slice a 1½" strip of patterned paper; vertically mount at right side of matted patterned paper background. Cut large circle from gold paper; embellish edges with swirl, fleur-de-lis and border punched shapes punched from matted gold cardstock. Cut smaller circle from beige cardstock for watch face. Layer gold sticker strips into Roman numerals around clock face; heat emboss small gold dots drawn with watermark pen between numbers. Attach gold clock hands with brad at center of clock face. Cut oval and arched window for photo and journaling. Complete clock face with gold letter stickers and punched border design. Assemble interactive spinning wheel with photos (following directions on template package). Freehand cut top of timepiece from gold cardstock; texture with paper crimper before layering over large oval ring with self-adhesive foam spacers. Oval cut 15 rings using cutting system; slice each ring at one end and link together on page. Oval cut fob from rust and gold cardstock; hang from chain. Embellish with fleur-de-lis and border design punched shapes; adhere sticker numbers at center of framed oval. Mount sheer gold ribbon across bottom of page, securing ends on back. Print title on red cardstock; silhouette cut and mat on burgundy cardstock. Silhouette cut again and mount on sheer ribbon strip intertwined with gold embroidery thread. Snip backs off of decorative gold buttons and mount on sheer ribbon strip.

Katherine Brooks

Greener Grass

Add a bit of shine with metal details

Katherine creates a textured background by rubbing metallic pearl colorant over a photo mat. Double mat photo on coral cardstock and textured cardstock. Texture second photo mat by laying tulle on coral cardstock collaged with patterned paper strip. Brush on a thin layer of liquid adhesive; dry. Add pigment paint over mounted tulle. Mount matted photo on textured mat; attach eyelets on either side of matted photo. String knotted wire through eyelets, securing at back of matting. Cut tag from patterned paper; press edges on ink pad to shade. Attach eyelet at one end and tie with fibers. Layer small date stamped tag, square punched photo and handmade tag under wire on matted photo. Print journaling on vellum; cut to size and tear one edge. Vertically mount at right side of matted red cardstock background with small eyelets. Slice a $^{3}/_{8}$" photo strip; ink edges. Mount over torn journaling strip with small brads. Cut vellum out of metal-rimmed tag. Press frame on embossing pad; sprinkle with gold embossing powder. Heat emboss with embossing gun. Print title on vellum; cut to size and layer with cropped photo under embossed metal tag rim. Attach eyelet and tie with fibers. Tie letter charm to fiber.

I Hope You'll Always...

Reflect color and light with metallic embellishments

Trudy's combination of metallic embellishments reflects color and light, adding dramatic dimensional interest to her page. Machine stitch sheer lavender fabric over lavender cardstock around edges; mat on white cardstock for background. Punch or cut squares into spring roll strip; machine stitch spring roll around edges near bottom of page as shown. String metal flowers with fibers, attaching bead through center of flower. Mount

strung flowers and fibers atop spring roll border, centering flowers in punched window; secure flowers with glue dots. Stamp name on small white cardstock strip with lavender ink; slide into clear plastic tab and set aside. Mat photo on white cardstock; lightly adhere on background to determine placement and measure for machine stitched border. Remove matted photo; machine stitch border. Cut material away from inside of machine stitched border with sharp scissors. Mount matted photo with photo corners inside stitching lines where material has been cut away; layer on page over clear tab and purple vellum die-cut flower embellished with bead. Stamp date on background next to photo. Craft dragonfly from wire and beads; mount at side of photo. Slice a 4"-wide strip of lavender cardstock; layer with white mesh and mat on white cardstock. Print title words on white cardstock and vellum. Paper tear edges of words on white cardstock; brush edges with purple chalk. Cut title word on vellum to size; attach to matted strip with eyelets. Mount metal letters over die-cut vellum flower. Stamp title word on metal-rimmed vellum tag. Die cut two small tags from white cardstock. Adhere sticker heart under glass pebble and border with black fine-tip pen. Attach eyelet and tie together with metal-rimmed tag; hang from metal letter "a." Mount spring roll scrap to second white tag; border with black fine-tip pen. Attach eyelet and hang from small brad with string. Attach metal letter snaps to tag and along bottom of matted strip.

Trudy Sigurdson

Birthday Tea

Detail photo mat edges with gold paint pen

Katherine paints photo mat edges with a gold leaf pen, adding a bit of elegant shine to richly colored papers. Print title; silhouette cut. Heat emboss with gold embossing powder before mounting over matted patterned paper background. Heat emboss swirl clip with gold embossing powder; when cool, mount over "i" in title word. Horizontally mount three photos on right page; horizontally and vertically border photos with ribbon strips. Mount brads at ribbon intersections. Tear patterned paper and green cardstock strips; layer and mount at lower corner of right page. Single mat two photos on green cardstock; paint edges with gold leaf paint pen. Let dry; mount. Triple mat one photo on green cardstock and patterned paper; tear bottom edge of second mat. Paint edges of last mat with gold leaf paint pen. Let dry and mount with foam tape. Stamp letters on small tag cut from brown cardstock. Shade edges with ink. Punch hole at top and tie with ribbon and string; mount tag at upper right corner of triple matted photo. Paper fold tea bag from vellum using template; fill with tiny circles punched from brown and tan cardstocks. Punch hole at top of tea bag, tie with string and wrap around bottom left corner of triple matted photo. Print journaling and date on ivory cardstock; cut journal block to size. Shade edges with ink. Press metal frame on embossing ink pad; sprinkle with gold ultra thick embossing enamel; heat emboss. Layer trimmed date behind gold embossed frame; mount on paper-torn corner with brads.

Meghan had been planning my birthday surprise for over a month. I was shocked that she could keep it a secret from me for so long, especially since I am known for never being able to keep a secret. To celebrate my 33rd Birthday Meghan brought me to Abbey Gardens for afternoon tea and lunch. I love anything old and Victorian, and the restaurant was beautifully decorated. I was delighted that Meghan shared my birthday with me in such a special way. I am very lucky to have such a thoughtful daughter to plan such a wonderful afternoon for her mother.

Katherine Brooks

I had a good friend who told me about this cute little scrapbook store that I just "had" to visit. Upon my first visit I was hooked!

Katherine Brooks

Kindergarten Hair
Keep it simple with silver accents

Diana's use of small silver brads works well with the simplicity of her monochromatic color-blocked page. Mount enlarged photo on preprinted patterned paper; attach brads at corners. Print title and journaling on vellum and preprinted tag die cuts. Write date on vellum; cut to size and layer behind silver frame mounted with silver brads. Cut journaling on vellum to size; mount on page with silver brads over tag detailed with eyelet and fibers. Cut title and descriptive words into strips; mount title word over enlarged photo with silver brads. Layer descriptive words printed on vellum over metal-rimmed tag layered with collaged colored paper strips; attach eyelet and tie with embroidery thread. Fold vellum envelope using template; attach eyelet. Insert written letter over patterned paper strip into envelope. Layer on page with silver brads over printed die-cut tag embellished with eyelet and embroidery thread. Cut journaling tag to size; mount atop photo with large brad allowing tag to move from side to side, showing hidden photo.

Diana Graham; Photos, Grins group Portraits, Palatine, Illinois

Diana Hudson

Too Two Cute
String stars on wire strand

Diana's freehand crafted stars dance across the page secured on a curled wire strand. Print journaling on white cardstock and part of title on blue cardstock. Cut journaling block into strip and adhere candle and present stickers at bottom. Mount two photos behind preprinted frames on blue cardstock background. Double mat two photos on white and blue cardstock. Freehand cut stars from colored cardstock to match design on preprinted frame. Attach eyelet at center of stars and border with colored pens. String wire through stars; curl wire ends and mount at center of pages. Unwrap paper yarn; mount on white cardstock. Cut title letters from paper yarn cardstock using template. Attach eyelet at center of "o" before mounting on page.

No More Training Wheels

Dangle an embellished tag from a beaded chain

Diana utilizes chains on her page to dangle a layered tag and link title blocks together. Mat green cardstock on blue cardstock for background; detail edges of green cardstock with black chalk pencil. Mat three photos on white cardstock; mount at left side of page. Mat single photo on blue cardstock. Print part of title and journaling on white cardstock. Cut journaling to size; detail edges with black chalk pencil. Attach four jump rings together; link to small punched hole in title blocks. Mat linked title blocks on red mesh. Cut journaling block to size; detail edges with black chalk pencil. Mount with red mesh scraps on tag cut from black cardstock. Tie red and blue raffia through punched silver circle at top of tag. Tie bicycle charm to tag with white embroidery thread. Cut large title letters from colored cardstock using template. Detail and shade edges of letters with white milky pen and black chalk; mat on black cardstock and silhouette cut. Attach red brad to top photo. Hang journaled tag and metal-rimmed tag layered with mesh and torn-paper scrap from beaded chain. Secure tag with glue dots over third photo.

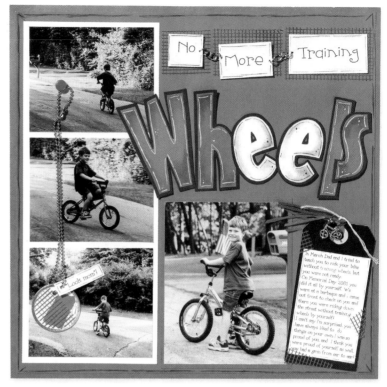

Diana Graham

Katherine Brooks

Play Hard

Mount metal title letters with brads

Katherine captures reflected light with metal title letters that pop off of a dark background. Cut window screen into 1¼" strip; mount at top of brown matted cardstock background with flat eyelets. Sculpt clay into stone shape; press letter stamps into soft clay and shade with metallic rub-ons. Mount metal title letters over window screen strip with black brads. Mat two photos on blue cardstock strip; mount at bottom of page. Mat one photo on blue cardstock; mount with self-adhesive foam spacers over enlarged photo sliced into 1¼" strips. Print journaling on vellum; cut to size and draw frame around edges with black fine-tip pen. Mount on page with tiny silver eyelets.

Through Great Love

Document a true love story

Torrey retells a memorable love story through journaling and an artistic assembly of metal letters and hearts. Cut squares and rectangles of colored cardstock into various sizes; layer over a white cardstock background. Print title and journaling on vellum. Cut title blocks to size; mount on page over cardstock squares with silver eyelets. Mount metal letters and heart shapes on page with colored eyelets. Bend wire into heart-shaped hanger to hold memorabilia; mount to page with "U"-pins and secure at back of page. Punch hearts from pink and blue cardstock. Layer with two-sided tape before covering with clear micro beads. Mount on page with self-adhesive foam spacers. Mat large journaling block on blue cardstock with eyelets; mount on page. Punch four more hearts from pink and blue cardstock; layer on border strip with metal letters and hearts secured with colored eyelets.

Torrey Miller

Grandpa's Girls

Clip fibers to photo

Brandi ties textured fibers to a swirl clip adding a bit of whimsy to a photo mat. Stamp designs on green and ivory cardstocks with watermark and colored inks. Tear edges of light green cardstock; crumple, flatten and layer together. Machine stitch on stamped green cardstock background. Mat photo on ivory cardstock; tear edges. Print journaling on stamped ivory cardstock; tear all edges. Machine stitch journaling block to page. Stamp design and title on metal-rimmed vellum tag; layer over ivory cardstock strip. Punch hole at side and tie with fibers. Mount on page with self-adhesive foam spacers. Tie fibers to swirl clip; attach to mat. Glue fibers into place.

Brandi Ginn

Alex at Beckwith Park

String metallic beads on a fiber border

Trudy strings metallic beads and weaves fibers into a beautiful border design. Tear large and small vellum strips; vertically mount largest strips at sides of pages as a border on matted green cardstock background. Create fiber design by stringing two fibers through one metallic bead, alternating and crossing fibers atop another. Wrap fiber ends around top and bottom of green cardstock; secure at back. Mat page with darker cardstock. Mat photos on green cardstock; mount over layered vellum strips. Print journaling on vellum; cut to size and mount at bottom of pages. String beads on fibers; feed through small pierced holes above and below vellum journaling blocks.

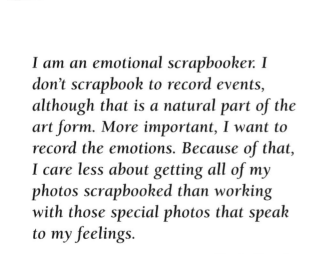

Trudy Sigurdson

I am an emotional scrapbooker. I don't scrapbook to record events, although that is a natural part of the art form. More important, I want to record the emotions. Because of that, I care less about getting all of my photos scrapbooked than working with those special photos that speak to my feelings.

Trudy Sigurdson

Tis the Season
Add shine with metallic tinsel

Holle's holiday page gets sparkle from wire and tinsel embellishments. Cut two 2½" strips of green cardstock; tear one edge and horizontally mount at top and bottom of blue cardstock. Die cut large and small title letters from gold paper and red cardstock. Mount green metallic tinsel at top right corner of page. Punch tags from dark blue cardstock; mount red title letters on tags. Punch hole; embellish and wrap with wire. Mount tags on page with self-adhesive foam spacers. Print journaling on ivory cardstock; cut to size and mount over red metallic tinsel with self-adhesive foam spacers. Complete page with pre-made 3-D embellishments.

We decorated our house on November 1 this year, very early because Thomas was leaving on December 4 for Kuwait. He was a great help getting the boxes down from the attic, helping me set up and decorate the trees, and putting lights on the outside of the house. I carefully placed the Santas Mama painted, set the table with Christmas dishes, decorated the top of the kitchen cabinets, bathrooms, and our bed. Thomas made the bed with our snowmen flannel sheets and helped me hang ornaments. Teamwork can ease the workload. Thanks Babe!

Holle Wiktorek

Heidi Schueller

Her Eyes, How They Twinkled
Hang tags and photos from sewing notions

Sewing hooks and eyes are used to "hang" embellished tags and photos with fuzzy fibers on Heidi's holiday page. Punch swirls from tan cardstock; detail punched shapes with chalk: mount on tan cardstock background. Slice three ½" strips of red cardstock; horizontally and vertically mount as shown. Double mat photos on colored cardstock. Craft hanging loops by slicing ½ x 2" strips of cardstock. Fold in half over top of double-matted photo; punch hole through loop and photo mats with eyelet setter. Attach brad through hole. Feed fiber through loops; tie ends to sewing hooks attached to page with "U"-pins made from wire. Mount fabric Christmas trees on metal-rimmed vellum and colored tags. Attach eyes to top of tag with wire "U"-pins. String with fiber and hang from hooks attached to page. Print title on plain and yellow vellum; circle cut to fit inside round metal-rimmed tags. Hang title tags from top of page.

Christmas Eve

Embellish with sequins for sparkle and shine

Holle adds colorful shine to her page with sequined photo corners. Mat green embroidered cardstock with red cardstock for background. Mat photos on green vellum. Cut corrugated cardstock into 1½" squares; diagonally slice and mount as photo corners. Embellish corners with sequins. Cut a 1¾" strip of corrugated cardstock for title block; tear top edge. Mount die-cut title letters and embellish with sequins. Print journaling on green vellum; cut to size. Mount one journaling block on left page with red and holly-shaped eyelets at corners. Mount second journaling block on right page; border with red fibers. Embellish die-cut Christmas tree with sequins and star brad. Layer metal ornaments on red cardstock; embellish with twisted and curled red wire. Mount on page with self-adhesive foam spacers.

Holle Wiktorek

When I started teaching scrapbook classes at our local scrapbook store and at conventions, I found true happiness. I am constantly learning and staying challenged with new trends and techniques in the industry.

Holle Wiktorek

Additional Instructions

To My Beautiful Daughter

Embellish tags with pressed flowers and leaves (Page 10)

Delicate pressed flowers and leaves adorn Trudy's layered and stitched tags, lending an organic element to an outdoor portrait. Horizontally and vertically stitch a 2½ x 12" piece of vellum across bottom of purple cardstock background, forming pockets as shown. Mount sheer ribbon atop vellum pockets adhering to back of page. Vertically tear 3" strips of pink and purple cardstock; brush pink chalk along top, bottom and left edges. Layer atop another and curl right edges gently with fingers. Stitch to background cardstock along untorn edges as shown. Mat photo on dark purple cardstock; tear bottom edge of mat before mounting on background. Die cut six large tags; two each from white cardstock, vellum and lavender paper. Tear vellum and lavender tags into thirds. Layer top third of vellum tag and bottom third of lavender tag over white tag as shown; stitch around all edges. Mount pressed leaves and flowers on tags with glue dots; wrap tags with white floral wire. Mount silver eyelet at top of tags over punched purple rectangle. Tie sheer ribbon at top of tags to complete. Computer print title words on pink and white cardstock. Crop into geometric and tag shapes; detail with pink chalk and black pen outline. Mount silver eyelets and floral wire before layering on page.

Trudy Sigurdson

Oh Boy

Wrap a precut matte board with fabric (Page 30)

Diana frames an expressive photo of her son with a fabric covered matte board and unique matting that defines what it's like to be a boy. Wrap precut matte board with linen fabric; secure fabric to back of matte board with tacky tape. Print two copies of dictionary page containing "boy" definition from The Century Dictionary Online (after obtaining permission to copy the text). Mat photo with dictionary definition page. Print title words in red ink over second dictionary definition page. Cut to fit inside metal tag; tie metal tag with gingham ribbon around bottom of fabric frame. Mount frame to patterned paper background with strong adhesive. Adhere leter stickers to metal tag; mount to background with silver brads.

Diana Hudson

Frolicking

Frame colored tiles with metal conchos (Page 52)

Diana uses a simple embellishment to add a bit of color to sliced panoramic photos. Print journaling on textured paper for background. Vertically slice panoramic photo at random increments; reassemble across page, leaving space between each slice. Cut first and last photo strip into squares; mount on page leaving space for tile embellishments. Adhere letter stickers for title above photos as shown. Mount colored tiles to page with strong adhesive; layer conchos atop tiles piercing page with pointed ends. On back of page, bend concho prongs down toward page to secure.

Diana Hudson

Live, Love, Laugh

Tie rolled cardstock strips (Page 74)

Trudy rolls cardstock into unique embellishments. Crumple and flatten light blue cardstock; mat on darker blue cardstock. Machine stitch horizontally and vertically at 2½" increments and around edges. Gently curl torn edges toward inside of page. Mat photo on tan cardstock; mount on darker blue cardstock with torn edges. Print journaling on vellum; cut to size and double mat on brown and dark blue cardstock with torn edges. Machine stitch double matted photo and journaling block over mesh strips to page; gently curl torn edges. Punch small stars from tan and blue cardstock; crumple, flatten and outline with black pen. Layer stars on page near photo and on journaling block. Die cut small tags from blue cardstock; punch hole at top and tie with hemp. Mount heart snaps on tags and outline with black pen. Layer with wooden blocks stamped with title words. Die cut large tag from tan cardstock; mount circle punched from brown cardstock at top of tag. Punch hole at center of brown punched circle and tie with hemp. Layer tag with large punched star outlined with pen and mesh; wrap with hemp and attach metal heart snap. Mount on page with self-adhesive foam spacers. Roll 1¼ x 5" torn paper strips and tie with hemp; mount alongside double-matted photo.

Trudy Sigurdson

American Dreamers

Stamp and emboss a gold metallic frame (Page 96)

Katherine adds a textured touch to a heat embossed frame with stamped stars and letters. Mat navy cardstock with burgundy cardstock. Tear 5½" and 6" strips of patterned paper; horizontally layer and mount at center of page. Attach eyelets at upper corners of matted background; string with knotted gingham ribbon. Create photo frame by cutting a 7½ x 5¼" window out of a 8½ x 6¼" piece of cardstock. Press frame on embossing pad; sprinkle with gold and clear embossing powders. Heat emboss; repeat steps. While second layer is still warm, stamp stars and letters into frame. When cool, mount frame over photo with foam tape. Cut vellum out of metal-rimmed tags. Heat emboss metal rim with gold embossing powder. Print title and journaling on vellum; cut to size and layer with cropped photos under embossed metal tag rims.

Katherine Brooks

SUPPLY LIST

The following supplies were used to create the art featured in this book.

Page 10 To My Beautiful Daughter
Tag template (Accu-Cut), small tag die cuts (Accu-Cut), heart eyelets (Creative Impressions), dried flowers and leaves, cardstock, vellum, ribbon, floral wire, eyelets, chalk, black fine tip pen

Page 12 Until I Saw the Sea
Metal-rimmed vellum tags (Making Memories), textured cardstock, cardstock, vellum, mulberry paper, fabric, seashells, lace, ribbon, wire, beads, square punch, blue fine tip pen

Page 12 Deep Thoughts
Corrugated cardstock (DMD), die cut letters (Accu-Cut), stamps (Plaid), eyelets, netting, cardstock, vellum, jute, leather scraps, sandpaper, chalk

Page 13 Super Scrappin' Getaway
Cardstock (Bazzill), vellum (Scrapbook Sally), netting, hemp string, sand dollars and starfish (Magic Scraps), chalk (Craf-T)

Page 14 I've Been Working on the Railroad
Locomotive sticker (Mrs. Grossman's Paper Co.), train track die cut (Deluxe Designs), cardstock, jute string, eyelets, rocks

Page 15 Patriot
Patterned paper (K & Co), letter template (source unknown), tag template (Deluxe Designs), corner stamp (source unknown), cardstock, hemp string, fibers, nailheads, chalk, fabric tag

Page 15 Time
Mesh paper, clay tiles (source unknown), letter stamps (source unknown), cardstock, copper strip, eyelets, button, embroidery thread

Page 16 Garth, Faith
Star brads (Creative Impressions), shrink plastic (Grafix), clip art (clipart.com), cardstock, vellum, wire, eyelets, hemp string, jump rings

page 16 Gone Fishing
Corrugated cardstock (DMD), die cut fish (Creative Memories), cardstock, string, chalk

Page 17 Feed the Birds
Birdhouse die cuts (Heartland Paper Co.), heart punch (EK Success), cardstock, brads, eyelets, jute string, spanish moss

Page 18 Miss Aysha
Metal hearts and stars (Provo Craft), dried leaves (Nature's Pressed), key charm (Rubba Dub Dub), flat eyelets (Making Memories), hemp string (American Hemp), cardstock, eyelets, raffia, chalk

Page 19 Branded by the Effects of Nature
Patterned paper (Paper Loft), stamps (Hero Arts), tag template (Deluxe Designs), transparency (Pockets on a Roll), cardstock, vellum, eyelets, embossing powder, leather, button, twine, burlap leaves, metal frame

Page 20 Adonis Narcissus Diggs
Patterned paper (Keeping Memories Alive), wooden fence (Darice), cardstock, vellum, brads

Page 20 Queen Victoria's Memorial
Patterned paper (Colorbök), dried flowers and leaves (Nature's Pressed), spring roll (Magic Scraps), tag die cuts (Accu-Cut), hemp string (American Hemp), eyelets, buttons, pigment pen

Page 21 Mother's Day
Textured cardstock (Bazzill), mesh (Magenta) paper frames (Leeco), memorabilia pockets (Therm O Web), pressed daisies (Pressed Petals), vellum

Page 21 Captured
Patterned paper (source unknown), cardstock, mesh, satin cording, button

Page 22 Uniquely You
Patterned paper (Colors By Design), polymer clay (Polyform Products), stamps (Hero Arts, PSX Design), metallic rub-ons (Craf-T), cardstock, inks, brads, wire, ribbon, embossing powder

Page 22 Year of the Dress
Patterned papers and vellum (Over the River), dragonfly stamp (source unknown), flower punches (Family Treasures), cardstock, wire, balsa wood, hinges

Page 23 Pure Country
Patterned paper (Keeping Memories Alive), corrugated cardboard (DMD), lettering template (Scrap Pagerz), stamps (PSX Design), square tags (Making Memories), flat eyelets (The Stamp Doctor), embossing powder (UTEE, Ranger), cardstock, chalk, ink, square punch, paper clips, jump rings, staples, screen, hemp twine

Page 24 Full of Beans
Tag template (Deluxe Designs), polymer clay (Polyform Products), stamps (PSX Design), fibers (EK Success), embossing powder (UTEE, Suze Weinberg's), waxy flax (Scrapworks), screen (ScrapYard 329), paper yarn (Making Memories), cardstock, circle punch, brads

Page 25 Amigo at the Denver Zoo
Cardstock, pigment pen, latch hook rug, mesh

Page 26 Gardening 101
Letter beads (Westrim), seed beads (JewelCraft), cardstock, eyelets, chalk, red hemp twine, pressed flowers, wire

Page 26 Destin, Florida
Corrugated cardstock (DMD), sand dollar stamp and inks (Stampin' Up), letter stamps (Hero Arts, PSX Design), alphabet die cuts (QuicKutz, Sizzix), cardstock, sea glass, chalk, star brad, decorative sand

Page 27 Seeking Shelter
Patterned paper (Creative Imaginations), mesh (Magic Mesh), cardstock, wire, chalks, eyelets, jute string, self-adhesive foam spacers

Page 27 Fishing
Handmade paper (Graphic Products Corp.), corkboard (Magic Scraps), stamps (Hero Arts), vellum tag (Making Memories), stickers (Paper Adventures), brown mini bag (DMD), cardstock, fibers, buttons, fishing line, metal screen, swirl paperclip

Page 28 Pinewood Derby
Patterned paper (source unknown), pre-printed photo strip (source unknown), faux wood paper, die cut letters, scalloped circle punch, cardstock, square punch, eyelets, fine tip black pen

Page 29 Uninvited Grill Guests
Mulberry paper (Pulsar Paper), lettering template (EK Success), sticker letters (EK Success), paper yarn (Making Memories), cardstock, chalk, feathers, black fine tip pen, white gel pen, brown marker pen

Page 30 Oh Boy
Patterned paper (Chatterbox), square and oval metal tags (Making Memories), ribbon (Offray), letter stickers (Creative Imaginations), linen fabric, pre-cut matte board, silver brads

Page 32 And Tia Makes Three
Textured cardstock (Bazzill), textured gold paper (Emagination Crafts), transparency (IBM), die cut tags (Accu-Cut), mesh (Magenta), fibers (Rubba Dub Dub), buttons (Jesse James) cardstock, fabric, brads

Page 33 Letters to My Son
Letter stamps (PSX Design), cardstock (It Takes Two, Bazzill), mesh (Magenta), hemp string (American Hemp), fibers (Rubba Dub Dub), eyelets (Scrapbook Source), photo corners (Canson), gray ink, chalk, circle punch

Page 34 Pumpkin Patch
Patterned paper (All My Memories), tag (All My Memories), leaf punch (EK Success), cardstock, fibers, buttons, chalk, wire, square punch, eyelets, cork

Page 34 Witchie, Witchie, Screamie, Screamie
Patterned paper (Design Originals), tag template (Deluxe Designs), spider die cut (source unknown), cardstock, circle punch, sheer ribbon, chalk, embroidery thread, buttons, fibers, black fine point pen

Page 35 Arizona Fall
Letter stamps (PSX Design), metallic rub-ons (Craf-T), copper (American Art Clay Co.), leaf punch (Emagination Crafts), fibers (EK Success), cardstock, eyelets, chalk, brad, inks

Page 36 A Mother's Pride
Letter stamps (PSX Design), fibers (Magic Scraps, Rubba Dub Dub), envelope die cuts (Accu-Cut), cardstock (Bazzill, It Takes Two), vellum, eyelets, brads, shells, ink

Page 37 Within You I See Myself
Patterned paper (C-Thru Ruler), conchos (Scrapworks), transparency (Staples), stamps (Barnes & Noble), ink, embossing powder, eyelets, brads, picture hanger, wire, ribbon

Page 38 When a Child is Born
Silver hearts (Provo Craft), cardstock (Bazzill), mica tiles (USArtQuest), dried leaves and flowers (Nature's Pressed), chalk (Craf-T), buttons (Jesse James), paper lace, skeleton leaves, ribbon, photo corners

Page 38 The Perfect Dress
Die cut letters (Sizzix), patterned vellum (Anna Griffin), dimensional stickers (EK Success), letter stamps (Plaid), cardstock, lace, felt, embossing powder, sparkle yarn

Page 39 You Can't Hide Beautiful
Patterned paper (source unknown), silver framed tag (Making Memories), heart stamp (Hero Arts), small tag (DMD), cardstock, vellum, brads, embossing powder, pressed flower, ribbon

Page 39 Jenna
Fibers (Rubba Dub Dub), letter stamps (PSX Design), date stamp (Office Depot), photo corners (Canson), cardstock, ink, fabric, ceramic buttons, embroidery thread

Page 40 Muriel
Silk ribbon (Plaid), die cut letters (QuicKutz), cardstock, embossing poweder (UTEE, Ranger)

Page 40 Dian Frybarger
Cardstock, fabric, ribbon, buttons, chalk

Page 41 A Pinch of Sugar
Leaf and butterfly pattern (Lasting Impressions), patterned paper (EK Success), vellum tags (Making Memories), cardstock, ribbon, embroidery thread, brown fine tip pen

Page 41 First Grader
Fibers (Rubba Dub Dub), eyelets (Making Memories), patterned paper (K & Co.), slide mount (Scrapworks), cardstock, vellum, ink, gold leaf pen, brads, ribbon

Page 42 Spring
Patterned vellum (EK Success), embroidery stickers (EK Success), fibers (EK Success), tag template (Deluxe Designs), cardstock, eyelets

Page 42 How Sweet It Is
Patterned paper (Karen Foster Design), flower die cuts (source unknown), corner flower stamp (source unknown), flower eyelet (Creative Impressions), cardstock, vellum, buttons, embroidery thread, ink, fibers, straight pin, ribbon, paper yarn, mesh

Page 43 Love...
Printed vellum (Posh Impressions), cardstock, embroidery thread, chalk

Page 43 Do Not Peek
Alphabet beads (Darice), silver-edged tags (Making Memories), flower stamp (Hero Arts), versamark pad (Tsukineko), cardstock, vellum, chalk, embossing powder, buttons, ribbon, mesh, fabric, fibers

Page 44 Beach Bums
Patterned paper (Frances Meyer), seashell stamps (Hero Arts), letter stamps (Hero Arts), sea shells (Magic Scraps), fibers (Rubba Dub Dub), cardstock, ink, chalk, embossing powder, glass pebble, watch crystal, spiral paper clip, fabric

Page 45 Sailing At Lake Granby
Cardstock, eyelets, twine, fabric

Page 46 Zoo Crew
Lettering template (Memories to Keep), embroidery floss (DMC), cardstock, wire, buttons

Page 46 Funny Face
Letter stamps (Stampin Up!), square stamp (Hero Arts), frame (Making Memories), cardstock, ink, eyelets, fiber (Fibers by the Yard), buttons (Magic Scraps), square punch, metal

Page 47 Busy Bee
Patterned paper (Provo Craft), embroidery thread (DMC), bee and flowers (Provo Craft), cardstock, clip art title

Page 48 Memphis
Patterned paper (PrintWorks), ribbon (Robin's Nest), cardstock, vellum, eyelets

Page 49 Being Your Mom
Tag template (Provo Craft), seashell charms (JewelCraft), seagull die cut (EK Success), cardstock, vellum, eyelet, silver brads

Page 49 Smile
Patterned paper (K & Co.), cardstock, vellum, buttons, lace, fibers, chalk

Page 50 Dressing Alike
Patterned paper (Anna Griffin), fibers (EK Success), embroidery thread (Making Memories), dimensional heart sticker (EK Success), vellum (Autumn Leaves), buttons (Making Memories), cardstock, sheer ribbon, eyelets, straight pin

Page 50 Fringies
Beaded ribbon (Hirschberg Schutz & Co.), embroidery thread (DMC), cardstock, vellum, gingham fabric, fiber fill, colored brush pens

Page 51 To Dance the Dream
Snowflake stamp (Holly Berry House), fiber (On The Surface), cardstock, vellum, mulberry paper, pigment powder, glitter glue, embossing powders

Page 52 Frolicking
Textured paper (Bazzill), letter stickers (Creative Imaginations), mini tiles (Magic Scraps), square conchos (Scrapworks)

Page 54 Best Friends
Corrugated cardstock (DMD), die cut letters, circles, frames and hearts (Sizzix), fibers (EK Success), beads (JewelCraft), jewels (Westrim), sparkle powder, (Z-Barten Productions), flower brad (Idea Tool Box), swirl clip (Boxer Scrapbook Productions), cardstock, mulberry paper, tinsel, wire, mesh, cork

Page 54 The Dance of the Leaves
Tag templates (Deluxe Designs), buttons (Making Memories), cardstock, vellum, eyelets, chalk, fibers, embroidery thread

Page 55 Joy in Blytheville
Suede paper (Wintech), beads (JewelCraft), gold and silver paper (Canson), die cut alphabet (QuicKutz), "JOY" stickers (Meri Meri), holly leaf punch (Family Treasures), pine cone punch (Emagination Crafts), dimensional wreath sticker (Westrim), cardstock, glitter glue, eyelets, ribbon

Page 56 My Little Man
Transparency (IBM), fibers (Magic Scraps, On The Surface), buttons (Hillcreek Designs), star die cut (Sizzix), wire (Artistic Wire), cardstock, vellum, eyelets, embroidery thread, square punch

Page 57 Friendship Braids
Patterned paper (Creative Imaginations), beads (Rubba Dub Dub), slide frame (Scrapsahoy.com), letter stickers (Creative Imaginations), embroidery floss (DMC), cardstock (Bazzill)

Page 58 Light of My Life
Patterned paper (source unknown), die cut letters (Accu-Cut), eyelets (JewelCraft), metal and vellum tags (Making Memories), fibers (Cut-It-Up), cardstock, vellum, chalk, beads

Page 58 Flowers
Patterned and embossed paper (Anna Griffin), beads (Westrim), gold textured paper (Emagination Crafts), lettering template (Wordsworth), cardstock, vellum, glitter glue, brads, self-adhesive foam spacers

Page 59 A Treasured Time
Patterned vellum (Autumn Leaves), metal-rimmed heart tag (Creative Imaginations), heart charm (source unknown), key charm (source unknown), metal frame (Making Memories), metal letter (Making Memories), metal heart tag (Making Memories), photo corner stamp (source unknown), heart punch (Emagination Crafts), clear ultra thick embossing enamel (UTEE, Ranger), cardstock, sequins, button, ink, sheer ribbon, eyelet, chalk

Page 59 You
Patterned vellum (Paper Garden), beads (JewelCraft), metal-rimmed tags (Making Memories), fibers (Cut-It-Up), hearts (DoJiggies), flower stamp (Stampendous), cardstock, wire, sequins, embossing powder, small brad

Page 60 Bubbles
Patterned vellum (Wubie Prints), letter template (Scrap Pagerz), bubble wand die cut (Deluxe Designs), cardstock, watch crystals (twopeasinabucket.com)

Page 61 Bubbily Sudsily
Patterned paper (Paper Adventures), clear microbeads (Halcraft), silver metallic cardstock (Canson), cardstock, vellum, wire, beads, eyelets

Page 62 You Make My Heart Leap!
Patterned paper (Karen Foster Design), pre-printed die-cuts (source unknown), plastic frogs (source unknown), letter beads (Westrim), tag template (Deluxe Designs), transparency, cardstock, buttons, embroidery thread, eyelets

Page 62 Kids
Patterned paper (Provo Craft), mesh (Magic Mesh), dragonflies (Traditions), cardstock, vellum, twigs

Page 63 You Are My Sunshine
Beads (JewelCraft), sheer ribbon (Robin's Nest), buttons (Making Memories), metal-rimmed vellum tags (Making Memories), tag template (Deluxe Designs), letter stamps (Hero Arts), leaf stamp (Plaid), cardstock, vellum, mulberry paper, eyelets

Page 64 Making a Splash
Tinsel (Magic Scraps), glitter (Magic Scraps), vellum (Scrapbook Sally), square punch, circle punches, cardstock

Page 65 Jewel of the Pool
Beads (Halcraft), jewels (Hirschberg Schutz & Co.), eyelet (Creative Impressions), patterned paper (Cut-It-Up), lettering template (Scrap Pagerz), letter stickers (Provo Craft), paper-pieced mermaid (Cut-It-Up), metal-rimmed tags (Avery), vellum (Hot Off The Press, HOTP), cardstock, ribbon, foam board, transparency, circle punches

Page 66 Moo-La-La
Star jewels (Magic Scraps), square and round jewels (JewelCraft), die cut flowers (source unknown), cardstock, vellum, glitter

Page 67 Winter
Jewels (JewelCraft), beads (JewelCraft), shaved ice (Magic Scraps), patterned vellum (EK Success), snowflake stamp (source unknown), snowflake punches (Carl, Marvy/Uchida), cardstock, vellum, ink, eyelet

Page 67 Ayasha's First Day of School
Buttons (Making Memories), fibers (On The Surface), beads (On The Surface), wire (Artistic Wire), patterned vellum (Autumn Leaves), letter stamps (PSX Design), metal-rimmed tag (Making Memories), metal stars (source unknown), cardstock, ink, pencil crayons, fine tip pens

Page 68 Fish
Lettering template (C-Thru Ruler), texture plates (Fiskars), fishing pole and lures (Crafts Etc.), cardstock, jute string

Page 68 Sweet 'n Sour
Chopsticks (Pier 1 Imports), Chinese stamp (Hero Arts), fiber (EK Success), Versamark (Tsukineko), fortune cookie die cut (Deluxe Designs), cardstock, embossing powder, Chinese coins

Page 69 Swim
Beads (JewelCraft), wire (Artistic Wire), letter punches (EK Success), Versamark ink (Tsukineko), fish charms (source unknown), cardstock, embossing powder, hooks, marker, glue dots

Page 69 Bathtub
Ceramic tiles (Plaid), cardstock

Page 70 Baby
Patterned paper (Karen Foster Design), polymer clay (Polyform Products), metallic rub-ons (Craf-T), lettering template (source unknown), stamps (Postmodern Design), cardstock, ink, embossing powder, brads, wire

Page 71 Sea Glass Beach
Beads (Blue Moon Beads), patterned vellum (HOTP), memorabilia keeper (C-Thru Ruler), versamark ink (Tsukineko), shell stamps (JudiKins), dots stamp (Stamps by Judith), cardstock, wire

Page 72 Home
Patterned paper (Club Scrap), letter sticker (Paper House Productions), letter stamps (PSX Design), lettering template (Wordsworth), stamp (Club Scrap), glass pebble (Making Memories), metal letter (Making Memories), flower nailheads, clock charm, frame charms, cardstock, gold ink, matte board, ribbon, tassel, gold embossing powder, square and rectangle punches, eyelet, fabric

Page 73 He's Leaving on a Jet Plane
Patterned paper (Autumn Leaves), beads (JewelCraft), corrugated paper (DMD), alphabet die cuts (QuicKutz), alphabet pebbles (Making Memories), star brads (Creative Imaginations), cardstock, wire

Page 74 Live, Love, Laugh
Cardstock (Bazzill, Paper Adventures), letter stamps (PSX Design), small star punch (Emagination Crafts), large star die cut (Sizzix), heart snaps (Making Memories), tag die cuts (Accu-Cut), mesh (Magic Mesh), vellum, ink, hemp (American Hemp), photo corners (Canson), circle punches, chalk, black fine tip pen

Page 76 Maize Maze
Lettering template (Scrap Pagerz), cardstock, vellum, fibers, chalk, self-adhesive foam spacers

Page 77 Remember
Mulberry paper (Paper Garden), handmade paper (Graphic Products Corp.), letter stamps (Plaid), coastal netting (Magic Scraps), transparency, cardstock, black ink, fibers, walnut ink, chalk

Page 78 No Yucky Stuff
Die cut letters (Accu-Cut), velveteen paper (Wintech), cardstock; silver cardstock, vellum, brads

Page 79 Dandelions
Sun punch (Carl), flower punch (Emagination Crafts), small star punch (Punch Bunch), small flower (All Night Media, ANM), small leaf punch, cardstock, vellum, self-adhesive foam spacers

Page 79 Holle's Hobbies
Patterned paper (EK Success) lettering template (EK Success), tags (HOTP), large gold brads (ACCO), rub-on's (Lil Davis Designs), eyelets, chalk, twine

Page 80 Clara
Patterned paper (source unknown), corner punches (ANM), cardstock, vellum, decorative scissors, oval cutting system

Page 81 Peter Rabbit
Decorative corner punch (ANM), cardstock; chalk, black fine tip pen

Page 81 The View
Patterned paper (Chatterbox), mesh (Magic Mesh), sticker letters (EK Success), plastic window (Chatterbox), cardstock, vellum, dried leaf (Hirschberg Schutz & Co.), brads

Page 82 Wedding Memories
Patterned paper and patterned vellum (Anna Griffin), printed frame (Anna Griffin), gold marker

Page 82 Family
Patterned paper (Northern Spy), wire (Darice), cardstock

Page 83 Tia and Trudy
Letter stamps (PSX Design), mica tiles (USArtQuest), tag die cut (Accu-Cut), heart stickers (Colorbök), dragonfly charms (source unknown), metal star (source unknown), cardstock, photo corners, ribbon, glass pebbles; swirl clip, eyelets, skeleton leaves

Page 84 Trains in a Bubble
Flower, leaf and grass punches (EK Success, Family Treasures), cardstock, wire, train tracks (source unknown)

Page 85 A Sweet Proposal
Patterned paper (Colors by Design), fibers (Cut-It-Up), die cut letters (Accu-Cut), tags (Impress Rubber Stamps), cardstock, vellum, eyelets

Page 85 Tootsie
Flower punch (Family Treasures), decorative corner punch (Family Treasures), cardstock

Page 86 She's Got Personality
Patterned paper (source unknown), tag template (Deluxe Designs), letter beads (Westrim), vellum flower stickers (EK Success), flower eyelets (Doodlebug Design), cardstock, vellum, embroidery thread, beads

Page 86 Springtime Smiles
Patterned paper (EK Success), die cut letters (Sizzix), die cut frame (EK Success), fibers (EK Success), flowers and leaves

Page 87 Sugar & Spice
Patterned paper (source unknown), vellum accents (Cherished Memories), cardstock, mulberry paper

Page 88 Arrows Lacrosse
Letter die cuts (source unknown), cardstock, chalks, string

Page 89 Hoops
Letter stickers (Creative Imaginations), basketball stickers (Frances Meyer), cardstock, square punches, black fine tip pen

Page 89 Tough Yet Tender
Mulberry paper (Paper Garden), lettering template (Provo Craft), die cut letters (Accu-Cut), tag (Impress Rubber Stamps), cardstock, vellum, metallic rub-ons, eyelet, jute string, chalk

Page 90 Lucky Fish
Vellum (Paper Adventures), crimper (Fiskars), cardstock, chalks, brads, brush pens

Page 90 Reflections of Albuquerque
Cardstock, vellum, square punches, triangle and rectangle and circle punches

Page 91 Valentine's Day Weekend
Corrugated cardstock (DMD), die cut letters (Sizzix), lettering template (Cock-A-Doodle Design), buttons (Westrim), state stamp (Destination Stickers and Stamps), cardstock, chalk, cork, ink, fibers

Page 92 It's the Little Moments
Cardstock, clips (Scrapworks), fibers (Rubba Dub Dub), vellum, chalk, ink, brads

Page 93 Christmas in the Desert
Date stamp (Staples), small tag (American Tag), fiber (EK Success), cactus die cut (Deluxe Designs), cardstock, circle punch, ribbon, brads

Page 94 Friday's Child
Sparkled cardstock (Club Scrap), cardstock, vellum (Paper Adventures), heart punches (Emagination Crafts), chicken wire stamp (Art Impressions), watermark ink pad (Tsukineko), ribbon

Page 94 Our View of Canoeing the Okatama
Cardstock, square punches, letter stamps (source unknown), pigment powder, bone folder

Page 95 Grant's Farm
Stamps (Hero Arts), sun punch (EK Success), 3-D sticker (EK Success), ink (Tsukineko), chalk, buttons, wire, eyelets

Page 96 American Dreamers
Metal rimmed tags (Making Memories), eyelets (Making Memories), stamps (Hero Arts, PSX Design), patterned paper (K & Co., Mustard Moon), embossing powder (UTEE, Suze Weinberg), metallic rub-ons (Craf-T), ribbon, cardstock, chalk

Page 98 Sand Between Her Toes
Metal hearts (Darice), wire (Darice), beads (Blue Moon Beads), letter stamps (Plaid), cardstock, vellum, self-adhesive foam spacers

Page 98 A Cherished Love
Patterned paper (Anna Griffin), eyelets (Making Memories), metal clock (7 Gypsies), wire (Artistic Wire), letter stamps (PSX Design), flower punch (Family Treasures), pattern stamp (Anna Griffin), date stamp (Staples), tags (Making Memories), cardstock, ribbon, inks, brads, embossing powder

Page 99 Explore, Discover
Textured paper (Memory Lane), metal star stud (Scrapworks), metal letters (Making Memories), screen (ScrapYard 329) letter stamps (PSX Design), versamark ink (Tsukineko), cardstock, mesh, inks, brads

Page 100 Two Little Souls...
Metal frames (Making Memories), wire (Darice), patterned paper (All My Memories), cardstock, mesh fabric, bead

Page 101 Cherished
Pewter stickers (Magenta), pewter beads (source unknown), wooden blocks (source unknown), fibers (Rubba Dub Dub), photo corners (Canson), cardstock, vellum, skeleton leaves, brads

Page 102 By the Shore
Patterned paper (source unknown), metal letters (Making Memories), metal photo corners (Making Memories), metal frames (Making Memories), metal word eyelets (Making Memories), pail and shovel die cuts (Deluxe Designs), cardstock, decorative sand, glass pebble, chalk, mesh, paper yarn, eyelet, metal mesh, circle punch

Page 102 Grandma
Patterned paper (Anna Griffin), metal frames (source unknown), metal plaque (Boutique Trims), cardstock, vellum, satin ribbon

Page 103 It's Not Fair!
Eyelets (Doodlebug Design), pewter sticker (Magenta), wire (Artistic Wire), cardstock

Page 103 Fuzzy Caterpillar
Patterned paper (Creative Imaginations), metal photo corners (Making Memories), metal rimmed tag (Making Memories), metal screen (source unknown), cardstock, silver brads, beads, button, square punches, safety pin

Page 104 Topsy Turvy
Silver nailhead letters (JewelCraft), eyelets (Creative Imaginations), cardstock, window screen, stainless steel outlet cover, wire

Page 104 The Blues Diner
Rubber stamps (Hero Arts, Stampa Rosa-no longer in business), cardstock, vellum, embossing pad, embossing powder, sterling silver high gloss embossing granules, eyelets

Page 105 In the Pits
Stamps (Hero Arts), eyelets (Making Memories), fibers (Rubba Dub Dub), snaps (Making Memories), screen (ScrapYard 329), washers, cardstock, square punch, ink, brads, embossing enamel

Page 106 Giddy-Up
Letter stickers (source unknown), pre-printed die cut letters (source unknown), metal letter (Making Memories), pre-printed photo frame (My Mind's Eye), western charms (source unknown), 3 dimensional stickers (EK Success), barbed fence die cut (source unknown), pre-printed photo strips (source unknown), cardstock, silver beads, hemp string, fibers, small silver brads, self-adhesive foam spacers

Page 106 Riding the Range
Large and small metal hearts (Provo Craft), cardboard, cardstock, hemp string, chicken wire

Page 107 Fascinated
Velveteen paper (source unknown), pewter letters (source unknown), metal frame (Anima Designs), metal star, cardstock, ribbon, crushed velvet, silver brads, black fine tip pen

Page 107 I Must
Patterned paper (K & Co.), brads (Hyglo/American Pin), swirl clips (Clipiola), copper strip (Art Emboss), walnut ink (Postmodern Design), cardstock, jump rings, microbeads, inks

Page 108 Looking Spectacular
Eyelets, brads, wire (Artistic Wire), die cut letters (Accu-Cut), cardstock

Page 109 What You Do At 2
Metal plaque (Boutique Trims), paper clip (Scrap Arts), stamp (Hero Arts), fibers, ink, cardstock

Page 110 Father's Build Dreams
Leather handmade paper (Memory Lane), snaps (Making Memories), letter stamps (Barnes & Noble), square punch (Family Treasures), cardstock, inks, embossing powder, screen

Page 111 Haley
Wire (Artistic Wire), lettering template (Scrap Pagerz), decorative scissors (Fiskars), cardstock, copper embossing powder

Page 111 Timeless
Patterned paper (source unknown), gold metallic cardstock (HOTP), gold sticker letters (Pioneer), interactive template (Scrapbook Specialities), swoosh punch, fleur de lis punch, heritage border punch all (Family Treasures), gold sticker strips (Mrs. Grossman's Paper Co.), clock hands (Crafts Etc.) cardstock, gold buttons, gold embroidery thread, gold embossing powder

Page 112 I Hope You'll Always...
Wire (Darice), metal letters (Making Memories), metal flowers (Making Memories), metal rimmed tag (Making Memories), eyelets, brads, spring roll (Magic Scraps), fibers (Rubba Dub Dub), tags (Accu-Cut), beads (On The Surface), letter stamps (PSX Design), heart stickers (Colorbök), chalk, cardstock, fabric, ink, photo corners

Page 112 Greener Grass
Metal rimmed vellum tag (Making Memories), charm (Memory Lane), postalz (Art Accents), wire (Artistic Wire), embossing powder (UTEE, Suze Weinberg), date stamp (Staples), small pre-made tag (DMD), cardstock; vellum, fibers, ink, brads, tulle

Page 113 Birthday Tea
Patterned paper (Daisy D's), letter stamps (PSX Design), vellum envelope (Ink It!), swirl clip (7 Gypsies), metal frame (Making Memories), cardstock, inks, ribbon, thread, gold leaf pen, brads, embossing powder

Page 114 Too Two Cute
Lettering template (EK Success), wire (Artistic Wire), eyelets (Doodlebug Design), pre-printed photo frames (My Mind's Eye), paper yarn (Making Memories) cardstock

Page 114 Kindergarten Hair
Patterned paper (SEI), metal-rimmed vellum tag (Making Memories), vellum pocket, cardstock, vellum, brads, metal frame, eyelets, embroidery threads

Page 115 No More Training Wheels
Mesh (Magic Mesh), lettering template (source unknown), metal-rimmed tag (Avery), bicycle charm (source unknown), tag template (Deluxe Designs), cardstock, chain, jump rings, chalk, white milky pen, black chalk pencil, raffia, foam tape

Page 115 Play Hard
Letter stamps (Barnes & Noble), eyelets (Making Memories), brads (Hyglo/AmericanPin), snaps (Making Memories), metallic rub-ons (Craf-T), polymer clay (Polyform Products), cardstock, vellum, embossing powder, screen

Page 116 Through Great Love
Metal letters (Making Memories), metal heart eyelets (Making Memories), wire (Artistic Wire), heart punch (Emagination Crafts), microbeads (Magic Scraps), eyelets, cardstock, vellum

Page 116 Grandpa's Girls
Metal-rimmed vellum tag (Making Memories), stamp (Raindrops on Roses), cardstock, ink, chalk, fibers

Page 117 Alex at Beckwith Park
Cardstock (Bazzill), fibers (On The Surface), beads. vellum, embroidery floss

Page 118 Tis the Season
Gold paper (Canson), wire (Artistic Wire), metallic tinsel (Z-Barten Productions), die cut letters (QuickKutz, Sizzix), 3-D Christmas embellishments (Westrim), tag punch (EK Success), cardstock

Page 118 Her Eyes, How They Twinkled
Metal-rimmed tags (Making Memories), flat eyelets (Doodlebug Design), fabric trees (source unknown), swirl punch (EK Success), cardstock, vellum, chalks, hooks & eyes, fibers

Page 119 Christmas Eve
Corrugated cardstock (DMD), embroidered paper (Creative Imaginations), die cut letters (QuickKutz), silver ornament charms (Making Memories), holly eyelets (Eyelet Factory), star brad (Creative Imaginations), tree die cut (Deluxe Designs), metal charms (Making Memories), cardstock, sequins, eyelets, wire, fibers

Sources

The following companies manufacture products showcased on scrapbook pages within this book. Please check your local retailers to find these materials. We have made every attempt to properly credit the items mentioned in this book and apologize to those we may have missed.

7gypsies™
(800) 588-6707
www.7gypsies.com

ACCO Brands, Inc.
(800) 989-4923
www.acco.com

Accu-Cut® (wholesale only)
(800) 288-1670
www.accucut.com

All My Memories
(888) 553-1998
www.allmymemories.com

All Night Media
(see Plaid Enterprises, Inc.)

American Art Clay Co., AMACO
(800) 374-1600
www.amaco.com

American Hemp—a division of Earth Goods, LLC
(800) 469-4367
www.ahbetterworld.com

American Tag Company
(800) 223-3956
www.americantag.net

Anima Designs
(800) 570-6847
www.animadesigns.com

Anna Griffin, Inc. (wholesale only)
(888) 817-8170
www.annagriffin.com

Art Accents
(877) 733-8989
www.artaccents.net

Artistic Wire Ltd.™
(630) 530-7567
www.artisticwire.com

Art Impressions, Inc.
(800) 393-2014
www.artimpressions.com

Autumn Leaves (wholesale only)
(800) 588-6707
www.autumnleaves.com

Avery
(800) GO-AVERY
www.avery.com

Barnes & Noble
www.bn.com

Bazzill Basics Paper
(480) 558-8557
www.bazzillbasics.com

Blue Moon Beads
(877) 377-6715
www.bluemoonbeads.com

Boutique Trims, Inc.
(248) 437-2017
www.boutiquetrims.com

Boxer Scrapbook Productions
(503) 625-0455
www.boxerscrapbooks.com

Canson, Inc.®
(800) 628-9283
www.canson-us.com

Carl Mfg. USA, Inc. (wholesale only)
(800) 257-4771
www.carl-products.com

Chatterbox, Inc.
(208) 939-9133
www.chatterboxinc.com

Cherished Memories- no contact information available

Clipiola- no contact information available

Club Scrap™, Inc.
(888) 634-9100
www.clubscrap.com

Cock-A-Doodle Design, Inc.
(800) 262-9727
www.cockadoodledesign.com

Colorbök™, Inc (wholesale only)
(800) 366-4660
www.colorbok.com

Colors By Design
(800) 832-8436
www.colorsbydesign.com

Craf-T Products
(507) 235-3996
www.craf-tproducts.com

Crafts, Etc.
www.craftsetc.com

Creative Imaginations (wholesale only)
(800) 942-6487
www.cigift.com

Creative Impressions
(719) 596-4860
www.creativeimpressions.com

Creative Memories®
(800) 468-9335
www.creativememories.com

C-Thru® Ruler Company, The (wholesale only)
(800) 243-8419
www.cthruruler.com

Cut-It-Up™
www.cut-it-up.com

Daisy D's Paper Company
(888) 601-8955
www.daisydspaper.com

Darice, Inc.
(800) 321-1494
www.darice.com

Deluxe Designs
(480) 497-9005
www.deluxecuts.com

Design Originals
(800) 877-7820
www.d-originals.com

Destinations Stickers and Stamps, Inc.
(866) 806-7826
www.stateofminestickers.com

DMC Corp.
(973) 589-0606
www.dmc-usa.com

DMD Industries, Inc.
(800) 805-9890
www.dmdind.com

Doodlebug Design, Inc.™
(801) 966-9952
www.doodlebugdesigninc.com

DoJiggies- no contact information available

EK Success™,Ltd. (wholesale only)
(800) 524-1349
www.eksuccess.com

Ellison® Craft and Design
(800) 253-2238
www.ellison.com

Emagination Crafts, Inc.
(630) 833-9521
www.emaginationcrafts.com

Eyelet Factory (wholesale only)
(503) 631-8864
www.eyeletfactory.com

Family Treasures, Inc.®
www.familytreasures.com

Fibers by the Yard
(800) 760-8901
www.fibersbytheyard.com

Fiskars, Inc.
(715) 842-2091
www.fiskars.com

Frances Meyer, Inc.
(800) 372-6237
www.francesmeyer.com

Grafix® Graphic Art Systems (wholesale only)
(800) 447-2349
www.grafixarts.com

Graphic Products Corporation (wholesale only)
(800) 323-1660
www.gdcpapers.com

Halcraft USA, Inc.
(212) 367-1580
www.halcraft.com

Heartland Paper Co.- no information available

Hero Arts® Rubber Stamps, Inc.
(800) 822-4376
www.heroarts.com

Hillcreek Designs
(619) 562-5799
www.hillcreekdesigns.com

Hirschberg Schutz & Co. (wholesale only)
(800) 221-8640

Hot Off The Press, Inc.
(800) 227-9595
www.paperpizazz.com

Holly Berry House, Inc.
(719) 636-2752
www.hollyberryhouse.com

Hyglo®/AmericanPin
(800) 821-7125
www.americanpin.com

IBM®
www.ibm.com

Idea Tool Box, LLC
(801) 375-1164
www.ideatoolbox.com

Impress Rubber Stamps
(206) 901-9101
www.impressrubberstamps.com

Ink It!- no contact information available

It Takes Two®
(800) 331-9843
www.ittakestwo.com

Jesse James and Co.
(610) 435-0201
www.jessejamesbutton.com

JewelCraft, LLC
(201) 223-0804
www.jewelcraft.biz

JudiKins
(310) 515-1115
www.judikins.com

K & Company
(888) 244-2083
www.kandcompany.com

Karen Foster Design™ (wholesale only)
(801) 451-9779
www.karenfosterdesign.com

Keeping Memories Alive™
(800) 419-4949
www.scrapbooks.com

Lasting Impressions for Paper, Inc.
(801) 298-1979
www.lastingimpressions.com

Leeco Industries, Inc.
(800) 826-8806
www.leecoindustries.com

Li'l Davis Designs
(949) 838-0344
www.lildavisdesigns.com

Magenta Rubber Stamps
(800) 565-5254
www.magentarubberstamps.com

Magic Mesh™
(651) 345-6374
www.magicmesh.com

Magic Scraps™
(972) 238-1838
www.magicscraps.com

Making Memories
(800) 286-5263
www.makingmemories.com

Marvy® Uchida (wholesale only)
(800) 541-5877
www.uchida.com

Memories to Keep- no contact information available

Memory Lane- no contact information available

Meri Meri
(650) 525-9200
www.merimeri.com

Mrs. Grossman's Paper Co. (wholesale only)
(800) 429-4549
www.mrsgrossmans.com

Mustard Moon
(408) 229-8542
www.mustardmoon.com

My Mind's Eye™, Inc.
(801) 298-3709
www.frame-ups.com

Nature's Pressed
(800) 850-2499
www.naturespressed.com

Northern Spy
(530) 620-7430
www.northernspy.com

Office Depot
(888) GO-DEPOT
www.officedepot.com

Offray & Son, Inc.
www.offray.com

On The Surface
(847) 675-2520

Over The River- no contact information available

Paper Adventures (wholesale only)
(800) 727-0699
www.paperadventures.com

Paper Garden, The (wholesale only)
(702) 639-1956
www.mypapergarden.com

Paper House Productions
(800) 255-7316
www.paperhouseproductions.com

Paper Loft, The (wholesale only)
(866) 254-1961
www.paperloft.com

Pier 1 Imports
www.pier1.com

Pioneer Photo Albums, Inc.
(800) 366-3686
www.pioneerphotoalbums.com

Plaid Enterprises, Inc.
(800) 842-2883
www.plaidonline.com

Pockets on a Roll- no contact information available

Polyform Products Co.
(847) 427-0020
www.sculpey.com

Posh Impressions
(800) 421-POSH
www.poshimpressions.com

Postmodern Design LLC
(405) 321-3176

Pressed Petals
(800) 748-4656
www.pressedpetals.com

PrintWorks
(800) 854-6558
www.printworkscollections.com

Provo Craft® (wholesale only)
(888) 577-3545
www.provocraft.com

PSX Design™
(800) 782-6748
www.psxdesign.com

Pulsar Eco-Products LLC
(888) 295-9297
www.pulsarpaper.com

Punch Bunch, The
(254) 791-4209
www.punchbunch.com

QuicKutz®
(888) 702-1146
www.quickutz.com

Raindrops on Roses
(919) 845-1242
www.raindropsonroses.com

Ranger Industries, Inc.
(800) 244-2211
www.rangerink.com

Robin's Nest Press, The
(435) 789-5387
www.robinsnest-scrapbook.com

Rubba Dub Dub Artist's Stamps
(707) 748-0929
www.artsanctum.com

ScrapArts
(503) 631-4893
www.scraparts.com

Scrapbook Sally
(866) SBSALLY
www.scrapbooksally.com

Scrapbook Specialties™
(702) 456-6661

Scrap Pagerz™
(435) 645-0696
www.scrappagerz.com

Scrapworks, LLC
www.scrapworksllc.com

ScrapYard 329 (wholesale only)
(775) 829-1118
www.scrapyard329.com

SEI, Inc.
(800) 333-3279
www.shopsei.com

Sizzix
(866) 742-4447
www.sizzix.com

Stamps Doctor, The
(208) 286-7644
www.stampdoctor.com

Stampendous!®
(800) 869-0474
www.stampendous.com

Stampin' Up!®
(800) 782-6787
www.stampinup.com

Stamps by Judith
www.stampsbyjudith.com

Staples
www.staples.com

Suze Weinberg Design Studio
(732) 761-2400
www.schmoozewithsuze.com

Therm O Web, Inc. (wholesale only)
(800) 323-0799
www.thermoweb.com

Traditions- no contact information available

Tsukineko®, Inc.
(800) 769-6633
www.tsukineko.com

USArtQuest
(800) 200-7848
www.usartquest.com

Westrim® Crafts
(800) 727-2727
www.westrimcrafts.com

Wintech International Corp.
(800) 263-6043
www.wintechint.com

Wordsworth Stamps
(719) 282-3495
www.wordsworthstamps.com

Wubie Prints
(888) 256-0107
www.wubieprints.com

Z-Barten Productions
(800) CONFETTI

Index